HE IS ABLE

HE IS ABLE

W. E. SANGSTER

BAKER BOOK HOUSE
Grand Rapids, Michigan

PHOTOLITHOPRINTED BY CUSHING - MALLOY, INC.
ANN ARBOR, MICHIGAN, UNITED STATES OF AMERICA
1975

PREFACE

THE ambitious plan of this book was to prove the adequacy of Christ to all the problems of life, but the author is only too conscious how inadequate the book is.

Big problems are not easily treated within the limitations of one chapter, and Christ so far outsoars our thought that all our words fall short and one reviews them with the knowledge that the half has not been told. Yet it is more satisfying to fail attempting to tell of his love and effectual help than to succeed with some simpler task.

Four of my friends richly deserve my thanks: Mr. W. E. Smith, who has helped me in a score of ways and to the end of whose kindness I never come in sight; the Rev. F. B. Roberts and Mr. H. L. Gee, who have read the MS. and made many acute comments; and Mr. T. Cyril Ellams, who has served me yet again by reading the proofs.

My wife's help in home and work has been unfailing.

W. E. S.

SCARBOROUGH, ENGLAND.

CONTENTS

I

WHEN I SURVEY THE WONDROUS CROSS

AT the Annual Exhibition of the Royal Academy in London in 1917, Charles E. Butler exhibited a picture which has since become famous. It is called "King of Kings" and depicts Jesus Christ standing at the foot of his cross and receiving the homage of the crowned heads of the world.

It is a remarkable painting. Three years the devout artist labored at his task and produced at the last a picture which connoisseurs have not hesitated to praise and which has hushed into awesome silence simple souls in all parts of England. It was the dying wish of its creator that it should be taken from town to town and exhibited without charge to all who cared to come and see, and, through his canvas, it may be said of Charles E. Butler, as of other noble souls, that "being dead, he yet speaketh."

The central figure is the Christ himself, regal against the dark background of his rough-hewn grizzly cross. The defeated Prince of Darkness cowers behind him while the monarchs of the world press in to do him honor. Edward the Confessor kisses his pierced hand. Louis IX of France proffers his crown. Constantine the Great kneels beside King Athelstan. King Cetewayo of Zululand finds place beside Queen Victoria. Julius Caesar, Barbarossa, Richard Coeur-de-Lion, and Napoleon are all prominent in the adoring multitude. Altogether one hundred fifty-eight portraits are included and only two are not royal personages — George Washington and Oliver Cromwell. Yet the eye never really leaves the King of Kings and the vision of his thorn-crowned brow abides in the memory for many days. So luminous is the halo about the head that some people have suspected a light behind the canvas, but there is no light there. The luminosity remains a mystery. All the components are known but they do not normally yield the unearthly glory that Butler captured. He mixed his paints with much prayer.

.   .   .   .   .   .

Is it sacrilege to criticize a picture of this character? Does its subject and the manner of its composition lift it above all questioning? Perhaps it does. Yet it cannot be denied that some have found it sentimental and have even been distressed by a sense of incongruity. Nero and Jesus do not easily fit into the same picture. Louis XI of France and Charles II of England look more than odd in the posture of adoration. Their very nearness to the Holy Son of God bring swift to one's mind the vaulting ambition of Alexander the Great, the paternal failings of Frederick William I of Prussia, and the sensuality of George IV of England. It is inevitable that one should feel how far from piety many of these men were in their private lives and it is difficult to resist the appearance of hypocrisy. The things for which so many of them lived and died had more to do with the Prince of Darkness than the Prince of Peace.

Moreover, the accident of birth which makes one man a king and another a commoner receives a disproportionate emphasis here. To the discerning eye, men are not chiefly interesting as they are emperors or paupers but rather as they have grappled with the circumstances of life and found their way to God, to service, and to interior peace. The royal robe is all but irrelevant. A noble heart beats beneath this one, and a mean, lustful heart lies behind that. Not as kings but as *men* do they demand our notice; not by their office but by their needs are they really to be distinguished. The eye of Jesus, one feels, is not held by the crown on their heads but by the ache in their heart, and his eye is just as swift to the suppliant who wears no crown and carries no scepter. Half the picture begins to fade out. Jesus holds the center still, but in place of the strangely mixed company of monarchs one sees the broken, beaten, despairing souls from all strata of society making their way to the foot of his cross and seeking his aid.

.   .   .   .   .   .

Is he able? May *all* come? Can he deal with *every* phase of human need? There are those whose difficulties arise out of their body, the sick, the unemployed, the sex-obsessed. Can he deal with all these? In the days of his flesh, he had a special care for the bodies of men. Did his concern with those things end when a cloud received him out of their sight? Or does he still heal the sick, feed the hungry, and cast out the demon of uncontrollable passion from the heart of tempted men?

There are those whose problem is largely a problem of the mind: the worried man, the futile and frustrated members of society, the people whose minds are haunted by fears, and the bereaved and brokenhearted.

Hamlet speaks of

> "The heartache, and the thousand natural shocks
> That flesh is heir to."

He does not exaggerate. When we add the complex spiritual ills of our poor race, the egotisms and the jealousies, the lovelessness and loneliness, the absence of prayer, the pride, hypocrisy, and vanity: when we add also the little sins, which are so large in their entail of evil, the idle gossip, the tainted hint, the self-deceit and limited consecration, we wonder if even Jesus can possibly meet them all. We look at the infinite variety of human need and ask, "Is he able?" Can he deal with those problems in their simplicity, and can he deal with them when several are entangled together in one human life? Can it be said in sober truth that no one is outside the compass of his help, or have we to understand all these promises as the pious exaggerations of preachers and receive them, therefore, with crippling mental reservations? From the laden souls of thousands who have turned wistful eyes and weary steps to Jesus, this urgent imperative question bursts, "Is he able?" and back from the released, redeemed, exultant souls of as many thousand more crashes the triumphant answer,

> "He *is* able,
> He is willing, doubt no more."

All may come. All the "comfortable words" of the Holy Communion service are universals.

"Come unto me, *all* ye that labor. . . ."
"God so loved the world, that . . . *whosoever* believeth. . . ."
"This is a faithful saying and worthy of *all* acceptation. . . ."
"If *any* man sin . . ."

When the tide of the Spirit flows strong through the Church, her hymns have the same universal sweep. A Methodist hymnologist has said that a chapter could be written on Charles Wesley's use of the word "all." It recurs again and again in the songs which expressed the abounding joy of the eighteenth-century Revival, and the keen ear of the "world's greatest hymnwriter" [1] pressed the emphatic word into the emphatic place.

> "For *all* my Lord was crucified,
> For *all*, for *all* my Saviour died."

> "Grace for every soul is free,
>   *All* may hear the effectual call;
>   *All* the light of life may see,
>   *All* may feel He died for *all*."

> "*All* may glorify the Lamb."

> "And *all* shall own Thou died'st for *all*."

"All," "every," "any," "whosoever"—these and similar words beat through the hymns, carrying the stress and

[1] Cf. Canon J. H. Overton, *Julian's Dictionary of Hymnology*, p. 1257.

widening the appeal to the uttermost. Only one thing in the universe is more amazing to the hymn-writer than the wonder and wideness of that love: it is the hesitation of the world to taste and see. It staggers his mind and almost breaks his heart.

> "O that the world might taste and see
>   The riches of His grace!
>   The arms of love that compass me
>   Would *all* mankind embrace."

.   .   .   .   .   .

I pick up my pen, therefore, having no skill with a brush, to paint a word picture of the suppliants around the King of Kings. Much gazing on Butler's canvas has made me feel the need of this complementary sketch. When I survey the wondrous Cross I do not see him as the King of Kings but as the great Physician of souls: not beset with monarchs but surrounded by beaten men and women. Infinitely good and gloriously equal to every need, I see his gaze fall upon the sufferers and pierce to the marrow of their problem. I see also the very presence of Jesus beget a bold faith in their despairing hearts and, as his power and their faith meet, the ancient miracle is worked once more. They touch him in life's throng and press, and they are whole again.

It is a mixed company that hedge him in on every side. They have only one thing in common—a consciousness of need: kings and commoners, princes and paupers, saints and sages, fools and philosophers, they each know this: "All the fitness he requireth is to feel their need of him." Even this he gives. In his pure

16

presence the self-sufficient realize the emptiness of their souls.

This picture will be drawn from life. Testimony will have preference over opinion and the argument of fact will be given precedence to all other arguments. Jesus can do it. Jesus has done it. Jesus is doing it. Let us turn to our study with the plain witness of a man who weighed words and whose claim to be both a saint and a sage few would gainsay. Baron von Hugel said in 1911 concerning his contact with the religion of Jesus:

"I should not be physically alive at this moment, I should be, were I alive at all, a corrupt or at least an incredibly unhappy, violent, bitter, self-occupied destructive soul, were it not for religion—for its having come and saved me from myself—it, and nothing else; it, in place of everything else; it, in a sense, against everything else."

Jesus did it. Jesus!

II

WHEN WORN WITH SICKNESS

STUDDERT KENNEDY used to say that a man who was undisturbed by the problem of pain was suffering from one of two things—either from a hardening of the heart or a softening of the brain. And Kennedy was right. Everyone who is mentally alive, especially if he believes in a God of love, finds this problem difficult of solution. Because, it must be admitted, even by the keenest believer in spiritual healing, that some sicknesses are proof against every effort at cure. Neither the prayer of faith nor the skill of the doctor avails. The disease takes its dread, unhindered course, and love's only ministry is to palliate the pain. Even this is not always possible. One must sometimes stand by and see a dear one racked out of human shape, and yet be incapable of any useful service. Death is not the deepest mystery. We must all die. But pain . . . !

Sir Arthur Conan Doyle tells in his autobiography what it was that made him a materialist in early life. As a physician, he constantly saw sights which he could not reconcile with the idea of a merciful providence.

"I was called in by a poor woman to see her daughter. As I entered the humble sitting room there was a small cot on one side, and by the gesture of the mother I understood that the sufferer was there. I picked up a candle and, walking over, I stooped over the little bed expecting to see a child. What I really saw was a pair of brown sullen eyes, full of loathing and pain, which looked up in resentment to mine. I could not tell how old the creature was. Long thin limbs were twisted and coiled in the tiny couch. The face was sane but malignant. 'What is it?' I asked in dismay, when we were out of hearing. 'It's a girl,' sobbed the mother. 'She's nineteen. Oh! If God would only take her!' " [1]

There are some people so shallow of mind, or unfeeling of heart that they can chatter cheerfully even in the presence of a problem like that. Sometimes they prattle about a deficiency of faith in the sufferer and suggest that God would cure the whole thing tomorrow if only the subject would "believe." Is it possible that they do not know that some of the world's profoundest saints have had to walk this way? Sometimes they suggest that pain is an unsubstantial bogey of our minds, a mere figment of a diseased imagination, having no basis in reality and curable by some simple readjustment of our thought. Is it possible that they can look on an acute case of rheumatoid arthritis, a body twisted to inhuman shapes, or stand, in the last stages, by a cancerous deathbed and really believe themselves that this is some figment of a diseased imagination? The world does not doubt that it is a healthy thing to fill the mind with strong positive thoughts, to the exclusion of self-pity and hypochondria, but when that modicum of widely-received truth is carried over and asserted as a cure of pain and sickness as a whole, the mind rebels against such impositions. Not by the cultivation of superior forms of self-deception can this problem be

---

[1] *Memories and Adventures*, Conan Doyle, pp. 83 f.

solved. It must be faced in all its naked hideousness. Is Christ able to succor us when we are worn with sickness, when every known resource of healing, spiritual, mental, and medical, has failed? Can he keep us brave, if not blithe; at peace, if not in joy? Is he able?

We *know* that he is able. We believe that in the same way as human parents must sometimes allow pain and discipline to press upon their dearly-loved children, so must the gracious Father in heaven allow pain and discipline to press upon us, not in any neglectful and unloving spirit, but for some high and holy purpose known to him. Though he does not will the calamities, he wills the conditions in which these calamities are possible. We believe also that, when we cannot interpret the dark mystery of life, and God seems indifferent to our plea for explanations, it is not because there is no meaning in it, or because he does not know, or does not care. It is just because, as yet, our minds are too small, and we cannot take the explanation in. We have reached that stage in human development when we are able to ask the questions, but are not always able to understand the answers. God expects us to trust his love.

I remember that when my little son had a nasal growth removed he was between three and four years old. The little operation was being performed on a number of other children at the same time, and the surgeon's waiting room was crowded. Unhappily, the slight accommodation made it necessary for each little patient, as the operation was completed, to cross the corner of the room where the others were waiting to go in, and complete concealment was not possible. They heard the cries, and saw the blood, and a tempest of questions rose to my little son's lips. He said: "Must I go in there? Will the nurse be coming for me? Will it hurt? What is it all for?"

Well, what can you say to a child of three and a half? You cannot talk about tonsillitis, or lymphoid tissue, or septic infection. You must just fall back upon generalities. You say: "I must not save you from it, dear. You will understand some day. You must trust my love." And when the moment comes you put him firmly in the nurse's arms for an experience which you know will be painful and nauseating, but which, for the child's sake, you are determined to see through.

That does not seem to be an unfair parallel of how God deals with us. In the vast affairs of this universe we are old enough to ask questions, but our minds are not yet big enough to understand all the answers. God says, "Trust my love." Can we not trust him though he leads us in the path which is so darkly wise?

The time of suffering is not a time for speech upon the ultimate problems of the universe. It is a time for the upward look and trustful silence. Some people are so strong in faith and so sure of God that they can praise him in pain, and pass through the valley of the shadow with songs on their lips. But they are rare souls. For most people it is a time for mute obedience. To fashion a philosophy in such an hour is surely a mistake. If we make it for ourselves, in the time of our *own* tragedy, it will border on despair; if we make it for others, in the hour of *their* grief, it is likely that we shall treat their sorrow too light.

The puerile explanations which amiable people sometimes offer of the dark mysteries in a neighbor's life
are shallow indeed. I once heard a benign Christian
tell a mother bereaved of her only son that probably
God had taken her son away in order to make her more
patient. Both the mother and I thought that it was a
pitiful attempt at an explanation. The cure seemed
so dreadfully out of proportion to the disease. Those
who set out "to justify the ways of God to men" need
a greater equipment of heart and mind than finds expression here. Better, a thousand times, to hold one's
peace than press a motive on God which we would condemn in a man. Some day we expect to pass into
his more immediate presence. Can we not willingly accept the mystery of suffering in the meanwhile? Enough
light beats upon this dark path for us to pick our way.
For the rest, would it not be filial and faithful to wait
till we get home when he will tell us himself?

I remember that when I was a small boy it was ar-
ranged one year that I should go on a fortnight's holiday
with my school chums, and that no grown-up people
should come with us. To our youthful minds the ar-
rangement seemed ideal. On the night before the holiday began, I counted up my pocket money and came
to the conclusion that it was not enough! So I went to
father about it. He heard my reasonings with a quiz-
zical smile and murmured something about my ignorance
of the value of money, but I left quite cheerfully with an
understanding in *my* mind that a postal order would
reach me during the second week. And in three days
I was ready for the postal order, so I sent off a post card

to accelerate it. I do not now remember what I put on the card, but I know the *kind* of card it was. "*Dear Dad, S.O.S., L.S.D., R.S.V.P.*"

But this was the queer thing. No answer came. The first week ended and still no answer. The second began, and slipped away, and still no answer. My chums noticed my preoccupation and began to explain the absence of the postal order in their own way. One said, "He has forgotten you're here." I knew that was a lie: I knew my Dad. Another said, "He is too busy to bother with a boy like you." I knew that that was a lie also. A third one said: "What do you think yourself?" I did not know what to think. It was all mystery to me. "I'll wait till I get home," I said, "and he'll tell me himself."

And when I got home it was all said in two or three sentences. Though I could still feel the sting of it, the look in his eyes was enough. I saw how much he loved me, and what it had cost him to discipline his boy, and I have known the value of money ever since.

That experience of boyhood has been a parable to me. There are certain dark problems in my family life which I have never been able fully to understand. I had a little sister once, my only sister, the youngest in a family of boys, an angel child who lived nine years— nine years mostly of pain. Fourteen times in seven years she went to the surgeon's knife, until she had no form nor comeliness, and her face was more marred than any man's. At the last, she had to be hidden away. Five gaping wounds yawned in her head alone, and only the strong-nerved could dare to look on what was left of that dear disfigured face.

And some looked and said, "There is no God." And others, well-intentioned but hopelessly incompetent, offered the most shallow explanations. But I was dumb as a boy and I am dumb as a man. Some light shines upon these dark problems but no *complete* solution is at hand. I give to inquirers the answer which I gave to my school-chums years ago. "I'll wait till I get home and he'll tell me himself."

> "Some day the silver cord will break,
>   And I no more as now shall sing;
> But oh, the joy when I shall wake
>   Within the palace of the King!
> And I shall see Him face to face . . ."

And he will tell me himself! In heaven! In the presence of those who came out of great tribulation! In sight and sound of the army of the redeemed! He will tell me himself. And I shall be *satisfied*, when I awake in heaven. Satisfied! [2]

Meanwhile, we are grateful for every ray of light on this dark path. It is not wholly dark. We see that, in some mysterious way, joy and pain intertwine. They are not really disparate; they belong together. It is a false antithesis which sets them one against the other. They often greet us on the path of life hand in hand. In joy were we conceived, but only by pain and labor were we brought forth. That godlike thing called mother-love was woven in woe.

[2] Cf. *Why Jesus Never Wrote a Book*, chap. 6; *God Does Guide Us*, chap. 10.

We see, moreover, how rich a service the sufferers render to our poor, tormented race. Sympathy is a shallow stream in the souls of those who have not suffered. There is something unheeding and harsh in a man who has known nothing of pain. And sympathy is far too precious in this needy world to begrudge the price at which it must be purchased. When Richard Baxter lost his wife, he declared, in his paroxysm of grief, "I will not be judged by any that never felt the like." It was only another way of saying that he could not be comforted except by those who had. Suffering, in a disciple, can often be wrested to service. It is Christlike work to soothe and sympathize, and only those who have drunk the cup of sorrow are fully equipped to do it.

Furthermore, as we come to understand the family life in which God has placed us on this planet, and glimpse the purpose which his loving heart is working out, we come to understand also why we are exposed to grief and pain. Some of it is begotten by ignorance and some by folly. Omnipotence could have avoided it all, but only at the price of invading our personality and making us marionettes. Can anyone, not utterly engulfed in sorrow, regret that God did not take that path, that his love would not compromise with sin, that he insisted that we bear the penalties of family life as we had enjoyed its privileges, that nothing would thwart him in his purpose of keeping us in those conditions by which we might attain to the stature of men? Fellowship with God is the fine fruit of this discipline.

"Nearness, likeness to our Lord,
Our exceeding great reward."

Is it worth it? Aye! Though seven deaths lay between.

Moreover, to some who suffer physical pain and bear the brunt of dread disease, this further joy is often given. Their sufferings help forward medical research. It may seem a very slight help, simply another one of a thousand "negative instances," but, however slight, if this were true, it would be vicarious. I believe that the mysterious malady which laid hold of my little sister has been better understood by reason of her seven years of pain. An eminent surgeon once said so. Perhaps others have suffered less because she suffered more. Sweet thought! It will add to the joys of heaven for her as she stands before the throne of God, with all those who came out of great tribulation, and serve him day and night in his temple.

Nor must it be forgotten by any who would have light on suffering that its power to curse or bless depends upon the reaction of the sufferer. Observant men in all ages have noticed that the same trouble in two lives has produced precisely opposite results. One is strangely sweetened, refined, enriched. Another is embittered, jaundiced, and made sour. The same distress! One suffered it willingly, dared to believe that God could wrest even from this ugly intruder something worth the price pain paid, sobbed it out on the Saviour's breast, but went on in brave faith. The other spoke bitter words, accused God, and took up arms against heaven. Even if the truth of their opposed

26

philosophies could be left aside as both, at present, unproved, one thing at least is proved beyond a shadow of honest doubt. The first live a happier, fuller, and much more useful life, and they are, moreover, much more pleasant to live *with*. Even if the reverent reasoning of the problem did not lead us to a willing acceptance of such woes as are, at present, inevitable, utility, other people's happiness, and our own peace of mind ought to do so.

I well remember a member of my congregation coming to my door one day in deep distress. Her daughter had recently been admitted as a patient to the eye hospital and had gone in with every hope of recovery. But the disease proved more deadly than anyone guessed and, on the day when my visitor stumbled over my step, the blow had fallen. The doctors foresaw that she would be blind in three weeks or a month and suggested that it would be best if the mother broke the news to her girl. She, poor soul, had come to pass the terrible task on to me. I went with lagging footsteps to the hospital, and I can see the little private ward now as I saw it then. The single bed, the locker, the polished floor, the drawn blind, and the patient turning her fast dimming eyes toward me. I talked of trivialities for some minutes, scheming for an opening, and half afraid that she would hear my thumping heart. Then she guessed! Perhaps I paused too long, or she divined it by some vibrant note in my voice, for suddenly she burst out with a half-suppressed sob, "Oh! I believe that God is going to take my sight away."

It was a hideous moment and an ugly phrase. My

divided heart in that minute was half in prayer to God and half in talk with her. I remembered a story I had heard of a missionary in India and what he had said when he lost his little girl, and I said, "Jessie, I wouldn't let him," and when she begged me to explain, I falteringly asked if she thought (not at once, but in three weeks or a month!) she could pray a prayer like this: "Father, if for any reason known to thee I must lose my sight, I will not let it be taken from me. I will give it to thee."

And in three weeks or a month she prayed that prayer. It was not easy. Does any half-wit think it was? One day she clutched at my hand and declared that she simply could not live in this world without a bit of light, but she offered the prayer before the last glimpse of day vanished forever. Peace came with the prayer. She carries the cross willingly, not grudgingly or of necessity, but with a cheerful courage. She is sweet to live with, and God uses her for the comfort and help of others.

The task of the minister is not easy. Every week brings its batch of difficult duties, and there are times when the spirit rebels. A succession of sad stories and constant contact with sudden tragedy and writhing pain drains one of nervous energy and drives one to perplexed prayer. Sometimes the prayers become complaints. We tell Jesus irreverently and petulantly that we cannot go to poor tormented people who are submerged in repeated sorrows and talk about a God of Love. And always, in such an hour, when the spirit is overwhelmed and the ministry insupportable, Jesus comes and shows us his wounds.

> "The dear tokens of His passion
> Still His dazzling body bears."

Poor dumb mouths! If those wounds could only speak . . . ! Yet, in their silence, they are mighty and draw the soul out through the eyes in hot, adoring love.

> "With what rapture,
> *With what rapture*
> Gaze we on those glorious scars."

It is enough. He is able! Able to succor the sufferers for he has suffered himself. Able to sustain his ministers and make them into living flame. Able to support the wavering faith of those who are tormented with doubt through all the long night in which the mystery hangs until, at last, he brings all his faithful into God's holy presence and in the light and joy of heaven the Father will tell us himself.

III

WHEN FEARS TRANSCEND

PSYCHOLOGISTS have often warned us against our misuse of the word "fear." They accuse laymen of speaking of it as an instinct whereas, of course, it is an instinctive emotion. They convict us of regarding it as a foe while all the time it is a friend. "If we only understood the service fear renders," they say, "we would never speak of it as an enemy again."

It is well to bear the warning in mind. Simple fear has been a faithful servant of mankind through all the long development of our race. Fear warns us against danger and checks impetuosity. Fear begets a proper care. Fear is the most efficient policeman on our traffic congested streets; it compels caution and preserves life. No man is without fear. If such a man should be born, he would be a danger to the whole community and a just object of dread.

Fear of the consequences is not the highest motive in rejecting evil, but it is a very common one and a buttress of morality not to be despised. In the hour of swift temptation, when desire and opportunity exactly coincide, many men have been distressed to discover that the love of virtue was not strong enough of itself to keep them in the paths of purity, but the fear of being found out checked the passionate impulse and saved them from disaster. None can doubt that fear is often a friend.

But it is a foe as well. Fear so soon becomes morbid. It ceases to be a cautionary mood and grows into a bogey that haunts the mind and finally enslaves the whole personality. It builds national barriers and piles up armaments. It hinders peace. It fosters racial hatred and plagues the individual life as well. Fear takes many forms. The fear of destitution haunts the honest poor. The fear of failure plows furrows in the face of business men. The fear of age fills the waiting rooms of plastic surgeons. The fear of death is almost as wide as mankind.

Can Jesus deal with fear? Is he able to deliver men and women from the paralyzing perturbations which make so many lives a burden? We answer without hesitation that he is able. There are no more exultant people in the army of the redeemed than those who have been saved from fear. "To be saved from the extremities of fear," they say, "is to be saved from hell."

.   .   .   .   .   .

So impressed are some people with the evil character of fear that they are disposed to make it the archdemon of all life and they say, "There is nothing to fear but fear." It is an exaggeration, but the exaggeration is pardonable. Many of our fears have no basis in reality. They are the homemade products of overanxious hearts and as unsubstantial as the Specter on the Brocken. The Brocken is the highest point of the Hartz Mountains in Germany. For centuries it was a place of dread because of the giant who lived upon its top. Many times had the giant been seen. Credible witnesses solemnly swore

31

that they had watched him, and people avoided the mountain as a place too dangerous to approach.

But with the advance of learning thoughtful men grew skeptical about the giant and made investigations. And this is what they found. They found that reliable witnesses had seen the giant only at sunrise or sunset— i.e., when the sun's rays were horizontal. They found also that he only appeared when the Brocken was free of cloud and when its neighbors were covered with mist, and they guessed the truth at once. The ghostly and terrifying specter which the traveler sees upon the sky is nothing but a magnified and distorted image of himself. He trembles at his own reflection. He flies at his own shadow. He thinks he is being pursued by monstrous and uncanny fiends, but he is being dogged by nothing but a diseased imagination. *Some* of our terrors are like that. They are simply not real. They are conceived and brought forth and nurtured in fear. Jesus sweeps that litter from our minds. The Specter on the Brocken disappears when the wind disperses the mist or the sun mounts higher. So do these unsubstantial fears vanish when the wind of the Spirit blows through them and the Sun of Righteousness appears. Have faith. "Fear knocked at the door, faith opened it, and lo, there was no one there."

. . . . . .

But not all our fears are unsubstantial. Fears are sometimes fostered by facts. A man living on the slopes of a volcano and constantly reminded of his peril by a pall of smoke and the shuddering earth has something more to fear than fear. He has facts to fear as well. Many people live in the shadow of ugly facts, and their fears have an undeniable core of truth.

Let us look at some of the common fears that not unnaturally haunt the minds of men and which are more than mere bogeys and phantoms.

There is the fear of *want*. How common this is and how old! Men have grappled with the fear of want from the dim dawn of history and, in this age of commercial depression, an immense multitude grapple with it still. Only those who have lived the life know the dread insecurity of living on an uncertain pittance, and the nightmare that life becomes unless those fears can be killed by perfect trust in the love of God.

Jesus met the anxious poor men of his day by pointing to the birds and flowers. "Behold the fowls of the air: for they sow not, neither do they reap, nor gather into barns, yet your heavenly Father feedeth them. . . . Consider the lilies of the field, how they grow; they toil not, neither do they spin. And yet I say unto you, That even Solomon in all *his* glory was not arrayed like one of these." So our Lord drew the inference. If God feeds the birds and clothes the flowers, he will feed and clothe his human children, who are of more value than birds and flowers. And seedtime and harvest have not failed. Though "man's inhumanity to man makes countless thousands mourn," God has been faithful. His general providence and his particular care have been constant through the ages.

Many are the incidents in the garner of one's own experience that confirm the promise. I have seen the strangest fulfillments of this word. Sometimes the answer to prayer has been so singular in its attention to detail that one could barely refrain from laughing, as Sarah laughed and St. Teresa and Henrietta Soltau. I remember the old saint who had been a nurse in an aristocratic family but found her pension insufficient after the war. One week she had to meet a bill of three pounds and had not so much as a shilling toward it. The thought of debt was dreadful to her and she begged God to undertake the burden and give her a settled mind. And, as she read the scriptures, a great peace fell upon her heart with the words, "Thou shalt have plenty of silver." Somehow she felt they were meant for her. She even declined a one pound note on the day before the bill was due because she could not feel that it was God's way of help. Then, in the hour of her need, when to some of her friends she seemed certain of disillusionment and not a little obstinate, her faith was triumphantly vindicated by the part repayment of a loan she had made to a neighbor years before and the very memory of which had almost slipped from her mind. Twenty-four half-crowns were put in her hand by an apologetic woman who begged to be excused for the delay and explained that only the most rigorous economy in her household had made possible the saving of an occasional coin. "Thou shalt have plenty of silver."

The old nurse laughed to save herself from crying, but the smiles and tears were all of joy.

Nor is that incident singular. Any man with ten years' experience of the care of souls could take out of his memory a group of little incidents of singular providence, differing in detail and sometimes so odd as almost to demand an apologetic preface, but *true*, as true as God and his love, and not easily waved aside as mere coincidences. For the most part they seem to come to people of great faith whose prayers are not compact of just petitions and who are very far from thinking of God only when they want something. But they witness impressively to God's personal care of his children and foster the faith in us which banishes fear. The recurrent needs of every day are all known to God. A full reliance can be put upon his promises. Many people know nothing of these extremities of need and must find God's providence work for them in ordered and unspectacular ways, but those who live on the lip of want may have this precious compensation that, again and again, from behind a frowning providence, clearer than their neighbors, they see his smiling face.

Or take another common fear—the fear of *bereavement*. This is an inevitable sorrow of life. All who live for any length of days come to a dark hour in a cemetery and follow as much as is mortal of some one dear to them. It is hard to keep this dread at bay because we know it is sure. I have a friend whose mother died when he was small and who is devoted to his father. His father grows old. Every new year my friend confesses to this fear. "I keep wondering," he says, "if father will be spared to me another year."

All folks know this fear in some form. Sometimes we pick up a newspaper and read of a terrible accident and the thought shapes itself in our mind, "if that had been my wife . . . or my child . . .," and we put the

35

paper down and think quickly of something else because our heart has turned sick inside us. The fear of bereavement is ugly, intrusive, and terrifying.

But, if bereavement is inevitable, we need not anticipate it. It would be the height of folly to mortgage the joys of halcyon days by importing a woe that may be far distant, and even if signs follow swift upon our fears and convince us that events will soon confirm our worst forebodings we still have securest refuge in the everlasting love of God. There is a special grace for a special need. That grace is not given with our anticipations: it is given only with the *event*.

Nor must the ground of this great confidence be confused with optimism. Mere optimism is a shallow delusion of the mind, absurdly overpraised. I remember once going to a family every member of which had been stunned by a sudden and awful bereavement and, try as I would, I could not pass God's comfort on. The words seemed to die upon my lips, and finally I murmured something about coming back later in the day, and I left the house. And at the corner of the street I saw a chirpy "wayside pulpit." It said, "Cheer up! It may never happen." I answered it back. I said, "It's happened." In a dazed way I kept repeating, "It's happened." There is no lift in optimism in an hour like that. Like the nerveless needle of a broken barometer it continues to point, even in a thunderstorm, to "very fair." It keeps saying, "Cheer up! It may never happen," and is utterly dumb when it does happen. The religion of Jesus says, "Even if it does happen—what then?" "Yea, though I walk through the valley of the shadow of death, I will fear no evil: for *thou* art with me."

Or take the fear of *age*. Folks often confess that this is one of their worst bogeys, and we all know people who are oppressed with the swift passage of time. I worked once with a man whose only reading matter was a book call *How Not to Grow Old*. His pathetic attempts to make a little hair go a long way and his childish glee if someone guessed him a couple of years younger than he was were pitiful to behold. He grew old rapidly. He was too anxious about it to keep young. Anxiety ages. His methods defeated their own ends like the usher in court who shouts, "Silence! Silence!" and makes more noise than anybody else.

Yet there is a deep and serious undertone in all this. Nobody wants to be a burden to others. Life grows wearisome to those whose powers are failing, and though we would never admit that our aged dear ones are a burden to us, we *do* find ourselves forging the hope that we shall not be a burden to those who come after us. Let us take refuge still in the love of God. Observations go to prove that it is possible to grow old gracefully and God has some rich compensations for his ripe saints.

Even when sight grows dim and hides the sacred pages, and hearing fails and public worship is closed as a channel of grace, he has his own secret ways of feeding our souls. I heard recently of a young man who had been in great trouble. His wife had gone blind. While her sun was still climbing the sky it was blotted from the heavens and midnight descended before it was noon. Her chief delight in life had been their lovely garden;

37

all her leisure was given to the cultivation of flowers and no small part of her bitterness arose from the thought that the garden had gone from her forever.

But her devoted husband has tried to give her the garden again and in a novel way. He has taken up all the plants that were there merely for their looks, and he has replaced them by plants whose chief merit is their smell. Out with the asters and in with the thyme. Out with the peonies and in with lavender. Out with the marguerites and in with stocks, pinks, and carnations. Out with the rhododendrons and in with more roses. And my last news of that heroic couple is that the wife has her garden again and her husband has the joy of giving it to her. By another sense she retains her own. Books are closed and life in the house grows irksome, but spring in the garden is still precious though the joy of it comes another way.

That seems to me to be a parable of the way God deals with his aged saints when their powers begin to decay. He finds a secret stair to their soul. He is constant when other joys have fled and he tells them things he does not tell to us. I am not disposed to dread old age when the saints open to me the treasury of their God-given wisdom.

Let the last word be about the fear of *death*. Few people are entirely ignorant of this fear in some form or other. Sometimes it is the physical fact of dying. Sometimes it is just regret at leaving so much that we have found beautiful and good. The thought of judgment is terrifying to others, while some shrink at the mere mystery of the vast unknown. If all these fears are matted together in one mind it invests the thought of death with unutterable dread.

On June 5, 1910, O. Henry, the famous short story writer, lay dying. As the shades of death gathered about him, he said to the nurse, "Nurse, bring me a candle." "A candle?" she said. "Why do you want a candle?" "Because," he answered grimly, "I'm afraid to go home in the dark."

Many people dread the path that leads out of this earthly life because it seems all dark. For them the great question remains

> "Whether 'tis ampler day divinelier lit
> Or homeless night without;
>
> And whether stepping forth, my soul shall see
> New prospects, or fall sheer—a blinded thing!
> *There* is, O grave, thy hourly victory,
> And there, O death, thy sting."

But think a moment. If God is our Father (and Jesus said he is), if we are among those to whom he gave power to become the Sons of God in all the richness of that relationship, and if death is but the summons to his more immediate presence, what room is there for fear? Most of us know that when we came into *this* world we were not unexpected and we were not unwelcome. Loving hands had made joyous preparation for our coming and warm arms held us tenderly against a warm bosom. Will our heavenly Father be less kind to us than our earthly mother? Is the love and hospitality of this poor earth more cordial than the raptured greetings of heaven? We cannot think it. "Perfect love casts out fear." "Love in its fullness drives all dread away."

We can but give the gifts he gave and plead his love for love.

IV

WHEN SORROWS LIKE SEA BILLOWS ROLL

Sooner or later all men and women need comfort. It does not matter how hard the man may be, it does not matter how composed and free from sentimentality the woman is, the time is sure to come when they will need comfort.

J. Pierpont Morgan, the American financier, was a hard man. His biographer says that the strongest quailed before him. His frown could cow the most ferocious and his eye was awful in anger. Yet when his wife died, his first wife, after scarce six months of married life, this hard metallic man was as one distraught and cried out for comfort. How human that is! Soon or late the need of comfort comes to us all. When that hour comes, however it should arise, where will we turn for comfort?

It would be folly to leave the quest to the hour. No man facing a grave operation remains uninformed as to the skill of the various doctors. His mind is fixed. When the time comes, he knows to whom he will turn. Do we know to whom we will turn when the need for comfort comes to us? Have we studied sufficiently to sort out the expert from the quack, the master craftsman from the mere bunglers? Who or what can mend a torn heart and make the mournful, broken hearts rejoice? Let us examine the different kinds of comfort that are offered to us and discover who is able.

Some men in sorrow turn to drink. I do not suppose that they theorize about it and weigh up one form of comfort against another. They want to forget and take what seems to them to be the easier way to that end. But it is a failure. In the first place it is horribly vulgar to soak in drink, and in the second place it is thoroughly ineffective. There is always the morning after—and then those poignant memories again. If they could forget forever it might be more understandable, but they wake up miserably sober, more than half-ashamed—and remember. It is a madness more than a method and can no more salve our sorrows than an anaesthetic can cure a cancer. Burns and Edgar Allan Poe tried it, and both discovered that it only aggravates the trouble it sets out to heal. No honest man really believes that he can find comfort in his cups.

Some people turn to books and recommend books and still more books to their sorrowing friends. "Find comfort in literature," they say. "The anodyne you need is reading; your cure will be found in a library." That was the advice that Edmund Gosse gave to his young friend Robert Ross when Ross was in need of comfort. He had become involved in the Oscar Wilde scandals that filled the newspapers in this country and in America in 1895. Gosse wrote him a letter of comfort and counsel and said, "Turn for consolation to the infinite resources of literature." [1]

Now the worth of that advice can only be judged

[1] *Life and Letters of Sir Edmund Gosse*, Charteris, p. 248.

by those who love books. People who have only a
meager interest in literature might wave this advice
airily aside and set the very slightest value upon it.
It must be judged by those who really love literature
and have garnered hours of rich enjoyment from the
printed page, who treat their books as they treat their
friends, who never cease to marvel at the privilege reading offers of hobnobbing with the great of all ages and
who put among their dearest possessions the well-
thumbed volumes on their shelves.

I count myself of that company, and yet I hold most
definitely, for all my love of books and all my deep indebtedness to them, that in an hour of real sorrow there
is no adequate comfort in books. When there is a
wound right across our heart, when the world has
grown suddenly gray, when ugly disappointment comes
and makes its home with us, books cannot solace the
desolate soul. You look at them but they seem strangely remote. They cannot reach the center of your sorrow. They are willing to give what they can but in
that hour you realize that they cannot give enough.

Is Dickens your favorite author? You will not find
him very gripping when the doctor is coming in and
out of the house and looking graver every time he goes.
Do you prefer Scott? The Waverley Novels will
hardly seem to be in the same world on the day you
come home from the cemetery. John Henry Newman,
the master stylist and superb litterateur, said: "There
has been a great deal of nonsense talked about the consolation of literature." Unquestionably, Newman was
right. He knew books if ever man did, and could write

43

English in a way that is the despair of most men, but he was sure that there had been a great deal of nonsense talked about the consolations of literature. It cannot be denied. Books are a glorious extra to those who know the real source of comfort, but they are absurdly remote from mending a broken heart. When Faber was dying he asked for the last sacraments and had to be reminded that they had already been administered. "You cannot have the last sacraments twice," they said. "Then if I cannot have the sacrament," he continued, "let me have *Pickwick*." A good book is a delightful extra. For those who are nourished on the richest food of the faith it is a pleasant sequel to the meal, but it could never take its place. When the children of my family were small we always had a chocolate after the midday meal. It was a pleasant little supplement, but it would have been a pitiable substitute. Literature is a supplement. For the real source of comfort we must look somewhere else.

Some people turn to nature. "Seek comfort," they say, "in the close study of this fascinating world and in the contemplation of majestic scenery." Sometimes they counsel us to study geology and zoology, and sometimes they declare that our healing is in the beautiful countryside. In so urgent a quest as we are pursuing, it would be unwise to neglect either aspect of this confident advice.

Lord Avebury was a champion of the former view. In the preface which he contributed to that fascinating two-volume work of natural history called *Marvels of the Universe* he said that science will do much to

44

"soothe, comfort, and console" the "troubles and sorrows of life." One turns with eagerness to any volume commended on grounds such as these.

Nor can it be denied that the study to which his lordship directs us is delightful indeed. From these varied pages I have learned all about the polycystins and the foraminifera. I have extended my knowledge of the dinosaur and the diplodocus, but for all the mental fascination of this study it is hard to find the consolation we were promised. If this is comfort, it is cold comfort. It may be true that any interesting branch of learning can serve to distract a tormented mind for a while but it cannot heal it. Certainly the study of these extinct creatures cannot cure. Indeed, I am not sure that they do not seem to stress the triumph of time over love and mock us in our loneliness and loss. Does all pure passion end in the grave? The diplodocus cannot answer. Can I hope for no immortality except to live again in minds made better by my presence? The pelycosaur cannot tell. Is this the most of comfort that zoology can give?—and can I be blamed if I turn elsewhere?

But nature has more soothing balm than this. Many advise us not to limit our study to natural history but to open ourselves to the healing touch of nature as displayed in the sweeping landscape, and all the moving loveliness of hill and vale and tree and flower. But it is with no better success to the real cure of our sorrows. No one will deny the joy of fascinating travel or doubt that God can use it to soothe a torn heart, but it is powerless to heal by itself alone. Indeed, the calm serenity of nature seems almost to rebuke our grief as childish. The hills cannot answer back. The stars can neither love, nor laugh, nor weep. They only shine, and they shine with indifference on our joy and our woe.

And if it be thought that the worth of this advice can only be judged by those with a high capacity for appreciation, let us call as a witness one whose sensitivity to natural beauty none can doubt but who discovered in an hour of overwhelming sorrow that even the melting loveliness of our English Lakeland could not mend a broken heart. When sorrow came to Ruskin he turned to nature, to the trees and the hills, the lakes and the lawns, but they failed to solace him. Beauty could not do it. There was no balm in Gilead. In the bitterness of his heart he said:

"Morning breaks as I write, along these Coniston fells, and the river mists, motionless and gray beneath the rose of the moorlands, fill the lower woods and the sleeping village and the long lawns by the lake shore. Oh, that some one had but told me in my youth, when all my heart seemed to be set on these colors and clouds, that appear for a little while and then vanish away, how little my love of them would serve me when the silence of lawn and wood in the dews of morning should be completed; and all my thoughts should be of those whom, by neither, I was to meet more." [2]

Oh, that someone had but told him in his youth . . . !

Some people in sorrow turn to art. They seek a panacea in music or pictures or sculpture, and it cannot be doubted that all these are welcome aids to those who

[2] I owe the quotation to the Rev. Dr. George Jackson.

know the secret source of every precious thing. Like literature and lovely scenery they are delightful supplements. But they can never be *substitutes*. They are not a fount of comfort in themselves.

The "Hallelujah Chorus" taken simply as music will not mend a broken heart. One will need to be convinced of the truth that the "Lord God Omnipotent reigneth," and it will take more than the music to do that. J. Pierpont Morgan gathered the finest private collection of art treasures in the world, but they could not satisfy him when the shades of death gathered about him. This bull-necked, bulbous-nosed, hard old man made his way to the house of God and sang with a full heart and moist eyes

> "Blest be the tie that binds
> Our hearts in Christian love."

Heine, the exiled German poet, loved all things beautiful, but he discovered the limit of its power to heal. He knelt in tears before the Venus de Milo, holding out vain hands to that serene torso, and cried, "It is beautiful, but it has no arms." Art has no arms to lift one up in life's bitterest hour. The most exquisite painting is a sublime irrelevance. The most finished statuary is chill. Art alone cannot succor, and if great art cannot do it, poor art cannot help. The man who modestly explains that, being no connoisseur in art he would turn for comfort to the cinema in any hour of sorrow, fosters a vain hope. If great art fails, poor art will not succeed. If God's own nature cannot save, Hollywood is helpless. If the Venus de Milo falls short, no painted film star can save. If Handel misses the mark, jazz is hopeless. There is nothing so hollow as simulated gaiety, and a breaking heart cannot long sustain pretense. Where is comfort? What sure word can be relied on when all the world has gone suddenly gray? Who is able? Who can heal?

Christ is able! Christ is willing. Let the broken-hearted make their way to Jesus. He, and he alone, has a word adequate to their need. No sorrow is outside the compass of his help. How tender he is toward those who suffer shame begotten by another's sin; the mothers who hide their face because of the wickedness of their boy; the sisters who seek to cover, like the Brontë sisters, the waywardness of a brother. So close he comes to tormented hearts in an hour like that and keeps them poised in a tempest of gossip. None knows more of the burdens of sin than he, nor how heavily the weight falls on those who were innocent of the great transgression. For this cause he endured the Cross, despising the shame, and as the comfort of his understanding sympathy seeps into the soul a new courage comes to face the world and to walk about among our fellows with quiet dignity.

And how tenderly he deals with those for whom life has been darkened by disappointment. He came to earth offering love, pouring it out passionately and prodigally on all who were in need, but, as month succeeded month in his ministry, his love found heavier burdens to carry. Cruel disappointments beat upon him. The crude ambitions of his disciples and the bigoted opposition of his enemies must have made life

48

incredibly lonely for him, but it could not freeze the stream of his love. Disappointment never made him sour. When, at the last, he stretched his wearied body on the cross, he knew what he was doing. Love had won a double victory. It had defeated the sin of man and the disappointment of his own heart. So he comforts the disappointed still and bars the way to cynicism.

Nor does he desert the bewildered souls who feel their prayers are all unheeded, who pray and pray for something that seems of certainty to be within the will of God and yet find the heavens as brass and are tempted to believe that God has forgotten to be gracious. Even this darkest of dark hours he knows. His piteous cry of dereliction on the cross makes him kin to all who feel themselves deserted and his glorious resurrection proves beyond all cavil that

> "Behind the dim unknown,
> Standeth God within the shadow
> Keeping watch above His own."

None can read the memoir of Allen Francis Gardiner, the intrepid missionary, without emotion. The story of his journey with six companions to Picton Island at the extreme south of South America is one of the most pitiful in all religious literature, and the beseeching prayers with which the diary of those starving men is studded is hard to read without tears. Their unburied bodies were found upon the shore when the belated relief ship finally arrived on October 21, 1851, and the last entry in the diary is dated September 5. But what an entry it is! Though the worst had come to the worst, the comforts of God were not absent. Gardiner writes: "Great and marvelous are the loving-kindnesses of my gracious God to me. He has preserved me hitherto, and for four days, although without bodily food, without any feelings of hunger or thirst." In the same simple and unshaken trust, we dare believe, he languished into life.[3]

Let our final witness tell of the comforts of Jesus in bereavement. If it is hard to meet untimely death, it is harder still to stand by and watch our dear ones meet it. Perhaps we never need the comfort of Jesus more than in that numb hour when we call our dearest by name for the last time and hear only the echo of our own voice. And while it would be invidious to imply that one bereavement is more bitter than another, it seems to some of us that no desolation is *quite* so terrible as that which falls upon a young husband whose wife dies as the price of motherhood. Can Jesus sustain a breaking heart and reeling brain in an hour like that? Let another missionary speak. John G. Paton was a missionary to the New Hebrides and took a young bride with him to his distant station on the island of Tanna. She died in giving birth to a little son, and seventeen days later the baby died too. Paton said:

"I was never altogether forsaken. The ever merciful Lord sustained me, to lay the precious dust of my beloved ones in the same quiet grave dug for them close at the end of the house; and in all of which last offices my own hands, despite a breaking heart, had to take the principal share! I built

[3] Cf. also Dr. Edward Wilson's last letter to his wife, *Wilson of the Antarctic*, p. 294.

the grave round and round with coral blocks, and covered the top with beautiful white coral broken small as gravel, and that spot became my sacred and much frequented shrine during all the following months and years when I labored on for the salvation of these savage islanders amidst difficulties, dangers, and deaths. Whensoever Tanna turns to the Lord and is won for Christ, men in after days will find the memory of that spot still green where, with ceaseless prayers and tears, I claimed that land for God in which I had buried my dead with faith and hope. But for Jesus and the fellowship he vouchsafed me there, I must have gone mad and died beside that lonely grave!" [4]

But for Jesus! When other helpers fail and comforts flee—there is still Jesus!

[4] *John G. Paton,* James Paton, p. 80.   Harper and Brothers, publishers.

V

WHEN IN LONELINESS

IT WAS May 22, 1913. The muddy Mersey was swollen
to full tide, and the gangways connecting the shore and
the landing stage at Liverpool were almost level with
the road. Ferry boats pushed their blunt noses across
the river to New Brighton and Birkenhead and, further down the stage, a prolonged bustle betokened the
departure of the SS. "Cedric" to New York. Rupert
Brooke, the poet, was aboard. He felt terribly lonely,
for no one had come to see him off. Everybody else had
friends. Excited groups of people surrounded him on
every side. He alone was alone.

Looking down on the stage from the deck of the vessel, he noticed a dirty little boy. Swift as thought,
he ran down the gangway, found the wee lad, and
discovered that his name was William. Brooke said
to him, "Will you wave to me if I give you sixpence,
William?" "Why, yes," said the little boy. So the
sixpence changed hands and the poet returned to the
ship to carry on a rather indistinct conversation with the
soiled but faithful William.

And presently the gangways were lowered, the ropes
cast off, and the tugs screamed out in their fussy fashion as they pulled the great vessel away from the stage.
And there, among the friends still left in England, some
of whom wept, and some of whom smiled, and some of
whom waved snowy handkerchiefs, and some of whom

waved hats, stood a dirty little boy, straining his eyes over the widening water, and waving a discolored rag. The poet's last comment on the incident was this: "So I got my sixpenn'orth and my farewell—Dear William!" [1]

Some people find it hard to understand a story like that. It seems to them eccentric behavior on the part of Rupert Brooke. "Only a fool of a poet would do a thing like that," they say. But to others the whole psychology of it is clear. They knew how he felt. It is awful to be lonely. How awful their critics have no idea. Born into a large family, blessed with the gift of making friends, coping all the time with a glut of social engagements, they do not know what it is to long for companionship and hunger for a friend. One wonders sometimes what they would feel like if circumstances cut them off from congenial companionship and they were suddenly to find themselves in the friendless environment, where some other people perpetually live.

Nor is the feeling of loneliness diminished if one finds oneself in the heart of a crowd. Indeed it is often strangely intensified. One can be *in* a crowd and not *of* it. When everybody else seems to have a friend, when there is the hubbub of happy chatter going on all around, the lonely souls who have no one to speak to feel doubly lonely, and almost wish themselves in a place where their friendlessness did not receive such emphatic proof.

Is Christ able to succor us in our loneliness? Can he enter deeply into a vacant life and understand the dull vacuity of days passed without a purpose? Is

---

[1] *Collected Poems,* Brooke, p. lxxxi.

the strong Son of God, on whom so much depended, able to meet the desires of those who feel that they have nothing to live for, and no one who needs them?

He is able!

He knew loneliness as no one knew it before or since. Greatness is always lonely. Great *men* have proved that. But who can conceive the awful loneliness of God incarnate among sinful men? So far as human understanding was concerned, he was lonely all his days. As a child he felt apart. He wist that he must be about his Father's business. When his ministry began it caused dissension and, finally, disruption in the home. Other men have known what it was to have all the world take up arms against them, but usually they have had some one at home who would take up arms beside them against all the world. Jesus lacked even that. His brothers and sisters came to believe that he was deranged; his sweet mother too. In what remained of his life, it was to his disciples that he looked for understanding, but he looked in vain.

On the eve of the Cross they argued about precedence; they slept while he agonized in the garden; when he was arrested, they ran away. It has been the comfort of martyrs at all times that somewhere in the world there were those who sympathized with them and understood the cause for which they died. Even this was denied Jesus. His sacrifice mystified the people who loved him most. It mattered to all the world that he died for love, but no single soul in the world understood that he was doing it. When the disciples heard in their hiding places that he was crucified they were dumb with bewilderment. They had seen him heal the sick, feed the thousands, and raise the dead, and now he let them drive great nails through his hands and feet and hammer him to a cross.

No one understood him. No one on earth approved. He was lonely with the awful loneliness of God. Can it be doubted that he can succor the lonely still?

The service of Jesus to lonely people takes a dual form. He can make them wise to enjoy the unspeakable privilege of companionship with God, and he can make them artists in human friendship as well. He can do both. To be open to this double ministry of Jesus is to be delivered from loneliness forever.

Let us look first at the great service—companionship with God. Jesus lived in the full enjoyment of his Father's presence through all the days of his flesh. When we speak of Christ's loneliness, we are thinking strictly of human fellowship. When Jesus slipped away from the crowds, and the inconsequential chatter of the disciples, for what we are pleased to call the "lonely nights in the hills," he was seeking uninterrupted communion with his Father. They were his feast times. In freedom from human companionship, he entered more deeply into the divine.

He has no more precious secret to impart to his disciples than this. To enjoy the presence of God, to live in his conscious nearness, to spend our days in reverent intimacy with heaven, is to live indeed. No one complains much of loneliness, however separate from his fellows he may be, if he uses his solitude to get nearer to his God.

55

Indeed, it seems certain that a dread of loneliness is often a sign of spiritual disorder. Abraham Cowley says, "It is very contradictory in human nature that men should love themselves above all the rest of the world, and yet never endure to be alone." Why is it that we so dread solitude? The saints seek it. Spiritual vision comes in solitude. It came thus to Moses in the wilderness of Midian, and to Paul in the deserts of Arabia, and to anchorites and contemplatives in all ages. A man told me once that he could not understand why hermits did not go mad in their loneliness. He was sure he would have done so himself. What a lot that man told me about himself in that single remark! He knew nothing of rich solitude, nothing of what Jesus meant when he said, "Ye shall be scattered, every man to his own, and leave me alone; and yet I am not alone, because the Father is with me." He knew nothing of what Professor A. N. Whitehead had in mind when he said: "Religion is what a man does with his own solitariness."

A healthy soul is not afraid of solitude. It demands it. If we fear to be alone, we may suspect ourselves of spiritual immaturity. When our life is given to God, when a firm fence is put round a part of each day and kept for quiet with him, when we practice the presence of God and reach out toward him by imaginative faith, then we can enjoy holy communion. Thomas à Kempis says: "Jesus will come unto thee and show thee his consolation, if thou prepare for him a worthy abode for him within thee. When Jesus is present all is good, and nothing seems difficult. To know how to keep Jesus is great wisdom. Be thou humble and peaceable, devout and quiet, and Jesus will stay with thee."

It is true. He will stay in difficulty, in obloquy, and when one is deserted by all earthly friends. The lonelier the way that his service demands, the closer he will come.

F. W. Robertson, the prophetic preacher of Brighton, proved it. He was bitterly persecuted by fellow Christians for expressing views which are widely held today. He was a lonely man. As his brief life sped away, his friends seemed to become fewer, but his great Friend came closer than ever. Here are three extracts from his letters. How sad they seem with misunderstanding, but how confident in triumphant witness.

"I shall be left alone as my Master was. I am hated by some who loved me once, not for what I do, but for what I think. I have long foreseen it. And, knowing that the Father is with me, *I am not afraid to be alone,* though to a man not ungently made there is some sharpness in the thought." [2]

"I am alone now and shall be till I die, and I am not afraid to be alone in the majesty of darkness which His presence peoples with a crowd." [3]

"I am alone, lonelier than ever, sympathized with by none, because I sympathize too much with all, but the All sympathizes with me. . . . My experience is closing into this, that I turn with disgust from everything to Christ. I think I get glimpses into his mind, and I am sure that I love him more and more. . . . A sublime feeling of a Presence comes about me at times which makes inward solitariness a trifle to talk about." [4]

[2] *Life and Letters of F. W. Robertson,* Vol. II, p. 99.
[3] *Ibid.,* Vol. I, p. 187.
[4] *Ibid.,* Vol. I, p. 188.

What glorious testimony! There need be no utter loneliness in God's world. Christ walked that way that no man need walk it again. No old man straggling behind his generation, no lonely woman living her life in a little back room, need feel the desolation of desertion. God will live intimately with the devout in *any* circumstances. A visitor to the poorhouse one day sympathized with an old Christian gentleman who was an inmate, and said, "I am sorry to see you living in the workhouse." The old man drew himself up with dignity. "I don't live in the workhouse," he said; "I live in God."

But the service of Jesus to the lonely does not end there. That is his richest service, but not the only one. He not only instructs them in living with God. He makes them skillful also in forming friendships with their fellows.

Not all the lonely people are lonely because of devotion to the things of heaven. Not *many* are. Not a few are lonely by their own fault. The circumstances of life may have compelled them to live alone but, instead of fostering fellowship with others by hospitality and service, they have grown morose, shrunk into their shell, become critical and self-pitying, and unconsciously driven folks away. These are all sad by-products of loneliness. People laugh heartily at the common joke about old maids because everybody has met the frigid, vinegary woman, whose loneliness has made her bitter and repellant, and whose bitterness has made her lonelier still. It need not be. The spirit of Christ can keep people youthful at any age, and attractive in any circumstances. One has known unmarried women in middle life glowing with kindness and whose fellowship was in constant demand because of an understanding sympathetic nature and a readiness to be a friend to others.

That is the secret of it. In a needy world like ours anybody can have friendship who will give it. Emerson said it over seventy years ago: "The only way to have a friend is to be a friend." Discerning men had known it long before Emerson.

It comes dangerously near to self-condemnation to say that one is friendless. It begs the rejoinder: "Have you been a friend?" Christ enlarges our capacity for friendship. He increases our love, turns our generous thought out upon others, makes us unconsciously more attractive, and adds a charm that does not belong to nature alone. The Greek word χαρις, which is translated in the New Testament as grace, also meant charm. The grace of the Lord Jesus Christ adds charm to unlovely sinners. It lights them up from inside. Everyone has noticed how radiant two people become who fall in love and find their love reciprocated. The love of Christ irradiates this poor human nature more permanently than that and heightens attractiveness in many ways. His presence in the heart removes the barriers to fellowship. Pride prevented us enjoying the company of those we thought our social inferiors, but pride is banished now. Jealousy hindered intimate fellowship with our colleagues and those who surpassed us in similar tasks, but jealousy has perished in the fire of his love. Our bias to believe the worst of

59

people has been turned into a bias to believe the best, and fellowship flourishes in the atmosphere of expectant faith. So the circle of our friends widens. Love begets love. In this world's goods we may be poor, but we are rich toward heaven and affluent in friends.

And if love is the great motive and attraction, we can learn something also of method from our Lord's example. He could converse with anybody. People of all levels felt his attraction, and he met them just where they were: harlots and scholars, priests and publicans, fishermen and Pharisees. How few of us have that gift. Outside the circle of our own limited interests we do not find it easy to mix with other people. We excuse ourselves and say, "They were not my sort."

But those who come close to Christ are infected with his desire for fellowship. They seek it everywhere and become masters in the art of winning it. The saintly Bishop King of Lincoln had learned something of the secret from his Lord. He called it "playing dominoes." He contended that if you wished to win the friendship of people you must be prepared to meet them on their own level. He had slight patience with the learned if they paraded their knowledge and embarrassed an uneducated man with whom they were speaking. He said:

"If a plowboy presents a blank to you, it is no use you bringing out your great sixes of knowledge. You must begin by playing blank to him, and perhaps, gradually and in time, you may so lead him on and draw out something from him which will enable you to play your sixes."

He certainly played dominoes' himself. He could win and keep the friendship of all kinds of people, some of whom he met casually on a train. He felt akin to folks at all levels of life. He retained respect for and sought the company of those whom others had abandoned as useless. Whenever he passed the prison in Lincoln he took off his hat. If Jesus cannot make us all as skillful as he made Bishop King, he can make us vastly more expert than we are.

Let us conclude with a simple questionnaire.

Am I lonely? Do I lack the friendship of God? If communion with God is possible, what hinders my enjoyment of it? Is my life not given to him? Are no unhurried moments of each day consecrated to fostering his fellowship? Need I be lonely any longer?

Do I lack the friendship of my fellows? Is it my fault? Have I been a friend? Do I seek to serve others with pure motive and slip into their lives with some simple offer of help? Have I asked too much in return? Have I deceived myself into supposing that my loneliness was the result of some kind of superiority of birth, or intellect, or spiritual discernment? Is it possible that pride, or priggishness, or censoriousness, or self-pity, have kept folks away? Have I checked other people's advances with any shyness or brusqueness of manner? Am I willing for Christ to put me right?

VI

WHEN COURAGE EBBS AND SELF-COMPASSION RULES

"When sorrows come, they come not single spies,
But in battalions!"

So speaks the King in "Hamlet" of the rising tide of troubles which threaten to engulf Ophelia, and so speaks also the common experience of men. Most mature people have noticed it. Difficulties have an uncanny way of coming together. For a few years everything goes pleasantly. There is no serious sickness in the family; income can be made to balance expenditure; the children are developing in a most promising way, and the harmony of the home is undisturbed. One can meet the inquiries of old friends with the cheerful assurance that all is well.

And then, suddenly perhaps, the skies cloud over with thick and threatening clouds. The doctor is in the house with a grave look on his face, and he drops dark hints about the character of the illness. And then, as though that were not enough, business difficulties seem to shut one in on every side, and nothing works out just in the way that one had hoped until, at last, a sense of bewilderment settles on the mind and it seems as though some sinister power has one in its grip. Perhaps, at the end, there is a journey up the cemetery path, and one returns to the house and wishes that it were possible to die. No phrase comes to the lips but this: "Everything's gone wrong." The whole world has tumbled about one's ears and, looking back afterwards at those dark days, the greatest wonder is how one lived through them at all.

While most people admit the liability of troubles to come together, nobody can fully explain why. Some light is shed on the problem when we recognize how one anxiety may nurture another. If a man is out of work and his family is undernourished, they are more susceptible to sickness than would otherwise be the case. A long period of sick-nursing and perhaps a great grief at the end is often the cause of another illness, or even a complete collapse. The connection here is close and recognizable. But it is not always so. Mystery hangs about this strange rhythmic law which underlies all life, and it is seen not only in the orbit of the stars, the tides of the ocean, the coming and passing of the seasons, and in such changes as "the swing of the pendulum" in politics; it is seen also in the ups and downs of the normal individual life, and part of the art of living is to learn how to deal with oneself when the path leads down into the valley of the shadows and when darkness is thick all around.

Now, one of the greatest dangers which can befall any man at such a time is that he should lapse into a state of self-pity; that he should look so long and so intently at his troubles that he becomes a martyr to this most debilitating of mental disorders and whine his way through life constantly seeking an audience which will listen to the long tale of his woe. It would be hard to exaggerate the dangers of self-pity.

63

Sensitive people are most prone to it. They are easily hurt. Unless they have been carefully taught that sensitiveness is capacity for sympathy (of which the world stands in such sore need) and that their power to feel deeply themselves is God's equipment to feel deeply with others, they will be trapped into this miserable mood of complaint and whimper the days away. Moreover, self-pity invariably exaggerates distresses. Molehills are seen as mountains. Trivialities assume tremendous dimensions in this moaning mind. When the condition becomes chronic, sighs are called forth not only by the heavy blows of adversity, before which even a brave man might bow his head, but by absurd little inconveniences, barely to be mentioned as a trouble at all. John Wesley stayed once with a man whose chimneys did not work properly, and who was bothered at times with a down-draught which filled the room with smoke. "This is my Cross, Mr. Wesley," he whimpered. The blasphemy of it! To make a comparison between a smoking chimney and the Cross of Christ!

Self-pity steals a man's courage. It filches the will to win. It disregards the just place of discipline in this mortal life and assumes that we should spend our days upon a bed of roses.

It is a solvent of faith. It dabbles in doubt and finds constant occasion to suggest that God has forgotten to be gracious. It is ever ready to parade some grievance against Providence and is so self-centered that some petty personal problem is clearly regarded as a more serious difficulty to belief than a major tragedy in the life of another.

It exposes a man to temptation. If faith ebbs and a man can believe that the universe and all his fellows have conspired to do him harm, he is ready for anything. He who is scrupulously careful in his normal mind to do the right thing feels absolutely careless when he is in the grip of self-pity. In this ugly mood many men have made shipwreck of their lives.

Can Christ save us from self-pity? None better! One can comb the record of his days with scrupulous care and not find a trace of this unmanly vice. He suffered the cruelest treatment from his enemies, and from some he thought his friends, but his sensitive soul was never ensnared into self-pity. He saw all his problems in their true proportions because he saw them in the light of eternity, and neither faith nor courage wavered. How forgivable it would have been if, in the last few hours of his earthly life, betrayed, deserted, scourged, and spat upon, his mighty heart had burst, and some great cry of compassion had fallen from his lips. But you will look for it in vain. There is bewilderment in the cry of dereliction, and there is agony when he says, "I thirst," but there is no self-pity. Indeed, the selfless practice of his life is the whole motive of his death. His thought of others explains the death itself, and every detail of it. His thought is so little of himself that in the high priest's palace, and amid the raillery and abuse of the servants, he can turn to Peter, thrice-denying Peter, and save him with a look. His thought is so little of his sufferings that in the praetorium, almost with an air of detachment, he can discuss with Pilate his mission in the world. On the way to

Golgotha he can turn to the weeping women and chide their tears: "Weep not for me; weep for yourselves and for your children." On the Cross itself he prays for his murderers, makes provision for his mourning mother, and grants pardon to a penitent thief. A heart so occupied with love for others is secure against self-pity. That is the great lesson which he is able to teach. Self-pity is begotten by selfishness out of sensitiveness. He can inspire unselfishness. Unselfishness and sensitiveness beget sympathy.

Not that we would suggest for a moment that courage in adversity is found only in those who have been specially schooled by Christ. The Stoics scorned self-pity centuries before that Divine voice was heard by the Galilean lake, and there have been men of similar spirit in all ages. Who that has studied the portraits Rembrandt painted of himself in the last years of his life can doubt it? Repeated blows had fallen upon him. Saskia, his beloved wife, died in 1642. Fourteen years later he went bankrupt. His priceless collections were sold for a song in 1657 and 1658. He was so poor at the last, Baldinucci tells us, that "when he was painting at his easel he had come to wipe his brushes on the hinder portions of his dress." When he died, no one among his contemporaries seems even to have noticed it.

But look at the self-portraits he painted in his last years. There is not a trace of self-pity in them. There is a touch of arrogance, and more than a touch of melancholy, but not a hint of self-pity. They are portraits of a man refusing to sink under misfortune. He seems to say, "Adversity may steal my status and my wealth, but all is not lost while I have courage."

Stoics are like that, for there is much in Stoicism that is admirable. Better a noble Stoic than a man who moans his way through life masquerading as a Christian. But better still a man who has so caught the spirit of Christ that he scorns the luxury of self-compassion and soars above that sub-Christian grace called "resignation," and cordially accepts the discipline of life, believing that God can wrest it to his good. Christianity and Stoicism unite in contempt of self-pity, but in place of the chilly acceptance of life which Stoicism teaches, Christ would make us wise to transmute it into something transcendently beautiful and can instruct us how, even, to *use* our woes.

Nor is it hard to quote instances of his triumph in this task. One thinks of St. Teresa in constant and cheerful conflict with ill health, battling all the time with her terrible headaches, those "rushing waterfalls" in the head, and with bouts of chronic fever, and at least one paralytic stroke. Yet nothing could daunt her courage or quench her gaiety. "When she thought how utterly out of proportion were the tasks laid upon her to her bodily strength, she would laugh to herself, so absurd did it seem." A smile and a jest were never far away. In 1580 she fell a victim to influenza, and under the awful depression which influenza brings even her conquering cheerfulness seemed to wilt. But not for long. When she shrank from the dreadful cold of a winter journey and was tempted to complain, the Voice said, "Do not mind the cold, I am the true warmth," and she went forth, as ever, with a cheerful courage on.

Catherine Booth was never well. She was the nervous child of a nervous mother and sickly all her days. In her fourteenth year her weakness resulted in curvature of the spine and she lay a long time on her back. Later her lungs were affected and it seemed likely that she would die of tuberculosis. Yet she lived to be the glorious mother of the Salvation Army and to do a work for God almost unparalleled in feminine biography. Two years of terrible pain completed her titanic life, pain which she would never permit to be dulled, despite her husband's pleading, by the kindly numbness of a drug. Looking back over the years, she could say upon her deathbed that she could not recollect a single day when she had really been free from pain. But it was said in no mood of complaint; self-pity had no part in her nature. Thankfulness and courage were with her to the end. The doctor who attended her at the last was an agnostic, and she was full of concern for his conversion. He said himself: "Her courage and anxiety for my welfare were beautiful." [1]

Nor is it hard to extend the list. Self-pity never made spoil of the noble Henry Martyn, even though he knew in the hot winds of the Indian summer that the dormant consumption in his system was taking him by the throat. He said himself:

"Study never makes me ill—scarcely even fatigues me— but my lungs! Death is seated there; it is speaking that kills

[1] *William Booth*, Begbie, Vol. II, p. 62.

me. Nature intended me for chamber-counsel, not for a pleader at the bar. But the call of Jesus Christ bids me cry aloud and spare not." [2]

He was a courageous soul. When he stood, completely alone, before the Vizier of the Shah of Persia, and was rudely commanded in the midst of the levee to recite the Moslem creed, "God is God and Mohammed is the Prophet of God," he cried out in the face of death, "God is God and Jesus is the Son of God." Cowardice and Christ do not go together. Suffering with Henry Martyn was not an excuse for complaints, but a mark of honor, and a ground of gratitude.

Francis Chavasse meekly bearing his humpback, Studdert Kennedy jesting at his asthma, the blinded George Matheson thanking God for his thorn, are all among the heroes of Christ's army. When Matheson took farewell of his Edinburgh congregation in 1899, he described himself as "barred by every gate of fortune, yet refusing to give in; overtaken by the night, yet confident of the morning." Self-pity has no place in true disciples. Like their Lord they have learned how to deal with thorns. They wear them as a crown.

Yet this quality of life is not found only in people who have won distinction. Thousands of obscure disciples display this same high courage. Every nurse knows the difference between the patients who are sorry for themselves and those who are not. The labor of the sick-room is not measured simply by the gravity of the illness, but also by the temper of the sufferers. One class of patients is harassed by the fear that they are

[2] *Henry Martyn*, Padwick, p. 229.

giving too much trouble and must constantly be reassured that they are not burdensome. They are clearly anxious to limit the labor of their illness as much as possible and are sorry for other people. There are others whose sickness is toil for several, whose demands are as incessant as they are trivial, whose recovery is delayed and service made heavy because they are deeply, and only, sorry for themselves. No nurse is in doubt as to which kind of patient she would rather serve.

Two simple thoughts kept constantly in mind will help our Lord to save us from this sin. Let us accept the principle of *discipline* in life. God has put us in a world where all kinds of distress can overtake us, where ignorance, folly, or sin (our own or another's) may provoke calamity at any time. It does not contradict his love; it is a condition of our freedom and a necessary element in our schooling. Let us accept it *willingly*. There is no situation out of which, granted our willingness, he cannot work good. Surely, therefore, self-pity is a mean and mistaken state of mind, and this personal commiseration must be abandoned. The place of disciples is in the company of those strong souls who, in every age, have borne the buffetings of circumstance with fortitude and cheerfulness and who say with Browning:

"I count life just a stuff
To try the soul's strength on, educe the man."

The second thought is this. An emotion, as the word implies, is a movement *outward*. Pity, therefore, should go out to others. It is perverted when it is turned inward and made into self-pity. We live in a love-hungry world, and a pity-provoking world: it is not seemly, or kind, or just, to expend our pity upon ourselves. It should

> "Raise the fallen, cheer the faint,
> Heal the sick, and lead the blind."

It should foster all fruitful philanthropies and never turn back upon itself.

I have a relative who went practically blind in early life. Just as his business was opening out, just as his children were getting old enough to delight in their father, just as his wife had taken to saying, "There are easier days ahead," he went all but blind. Midnight descended at noonday. He made terms with the inevitable, took a little place in the country, and faced the dark future with a stout heart. Even in the shadows he is a gay soul, and people have often wondered at his courage, but the simple secret is this. Often he recites Milton's sonnet, "On His Blindness." He cheers his own sad heart with the tonic words of the immortal singer. Few things are more moving than to see him stand and, staring out of his dimmed eyes, declare:

> "Who best
> Bear His mild yoke, they serve Him best . . .
> They also serve who only stand and wait."

That is the answer of the valiant soul to the devastating affliction, and it is magnificent. God grant him wider spheres of service when twilight turns to day.

71

VII

WHEN REVENGE MY HEART INVADES

Sooner or later, in this mixed world, everybody gets a hard knock. Indeed, some get so many that they are tempted to believe that life is made up of them and they cease to expect anything else.

The hard knocks are of different kinds. Some arise from circumstances, or the inevitable conditions of our mortal life, and no element of blame enters in. Accidents happen, mistakes are made, death strides in and deals a crushing blow, but these are not the hardest knocks that we endure. There is no evil will behind them. It is nobody's fault. It is a wound, a deep wound perhaps, but it is a clean one. There is no pus or poison in it. In course of time it will surely heal. The most difficult wounds, the wounds that refuse to heal and take a constant toll of health and strength, are the wounds deliberately given. The thrust that was meant to be a thrust. The injury consciously and cruelly aimed for. The stab that was planned and had venom in it. These are the wounds which hurt, and burn, and throb, and fester; which nurture the passion for vengeance and make one furtive, bitter, hateful. Many a noble life has been blasted by the longing for vengeance begotten, in the first place, by some savage injury or piece of malicious spite.

Does it surprise anyone if a man whose daughter has been foully assaulted should seek revenge upon the lustful beast who caused her degradation? Would a normal man have condemned Colonel Lindbergh if he had resolved, over the soiled body of his dear, dead child, to spend his days in seeking the dastardly murderer of his innocent babe, and never to rest until he had had revenge?

The passion for vengeance is grounded in human nature. It is a deep elemental desire, known to primitive and civilized men alike, and burns in the dark recesses of our hearts. It is a compound of wounded self-regard and anger. Through the long history of our race it lies behind the blood-feud; it has provoked wars; it is one of the chief sources of the institution of public justice.

The desire to "get even" with others, however, does not arise only in great injuries. It is provoked in some people by any deliberate wound to their pride, especially if it is delivered in public, and makes them the subject of scornful laughter. A snub, a piece of sarcasm, a contemptuous word, all these foster the desire in normal human nature, for some stinging retort. If the retort halts upon the lips, the incident is not forgotten. It is fostered in the memory, long after it has slipped from the minds of others, and men ferret about for the chance of revenge.

J. Pierpont Morgan, the American financier, was attacked in later life by a strange disease which showed itself most obviously in an enormous enlargement of his already prominent nose. He was one of the richest men in the world, but no specialist could reduce its size, and it hung like a monstrous bulb on his face, spotted

73

with red and purple marks. He grew very sensitive about it. Cartoonists sketched it, and rhymsters made verses on it, but if anyone made a ludicrous remark about it which came to Morgan's ears, he never forgot. Many a wit had to pay for his witticism. If they wanted to laugh at him, he fixed the price for the laugh. Small as the offense may seem, his wounded pride was never satisfied without revenge.

Who can deliver us from this elemental passion? Can anyone take from our hearts the slow, deep fire of resentment, and give us love in place of hate? Christ can! In the days of his flesh he said: "Love your enemies, bless them that curse you, do good to them that hate you, and pray for them which despitefully use you, and persecute you." Paul caught his Master's spirit and said, "Avenge not yourselves, but rather give place unto wrath . . . if thine enemy hunger, feed him; if he thirst, give him drink: for in so doing thou shalt heap coals of fire on his head."

Can it be done? Even with grace? Did the Master set an impossible standard and his servant make an unreasonable demand? Is this a counsel of perfection which we should salute but cannot hope to attain? Surely not! Hard as it is, it is possible. Strenuous though the spiritual discipline may prove, it is healthy. Foolish as it may seem to the wise ones of this world, it is wonderfully effective. Granted a consecrated servant, he can eradicate even the passion for revenge.

None will deny that to forgive is healthy. To bear spite, to plan reprisals, to live for vengeance is to nurture ill health at the center of one's being. Hate plays strange tricks with memory. It exaggerates the injury. It opposes time's healing touch. It curdles the milk of human kindness. It strangles the kindlier impulses of nature. It gives one a jaundiced outlook on life until one is shunned by others as a bitter and cynical soul. The men who have lived for nought but vengeance have made no contribution to the good of humankind.

Forgiveness, on the other hand, is rejuvenating. It has tonic properties for the body. It gives breadth and vigor to the mind. The soul it irrigates blooms like a well-watered garden. It is a wonderful experience to *be* forgiven, but it is not less wonderful to forgive. What a burden rolls from the heart of a conscience-stricken culprit convinced that the man he has injured has really forgiven him, but what a burden rolls from the heart and mind of the man who had been big enough to forgive. The passion for revenge is a poison. However deep the injury and just the resentment, the poison is deadly. It is deadly to the man who holds it. Forgiveness is the only cure.

But many people protest, even while they admit the benison of forgiveness, that it is not possible for normal men to forego revenge. They are probably right, so far as it concerns men who do not know the grace of God, but they are plainly wrong if they refer to those who do. It becomes a question of fact. Is it possible to cite instances of men and women who have risen to this supernatural level? Most certainly it is.

Mahatma Gandhi is not a member of the Christian Church, though those who know him best insist that the Spirit of Christ dwells in him. He has made no secret of his indebtedness to Jesus and the Sermon on the Mount.   He says: "It was the New Testament which really awakened me to the rightness and value of passive resistance, and love toward one's enemies.   When I read in the Sermon on the Mount such passages, 'Resist not him that is evil, but whosoever smiteth thee on thy right cheek, turn to him the other also,' or 'Love your enemies, bless them that persecute you, that you may be the sons of your Father which is in heaven,' I was simply overjoyed."

In 1908 Gandhi was attacked and nearly murdered by a fanatical Moslem, but he refused to prosecute his assailant or even give evidence against him.   On the day of the crime, and when he lay at death's door, he summoned his fast-ebbing strength to issue an appeal to his followers to take no steps against the man.   "This man," he said, "did not know what he was doing.   He thought that I was doing what was wrong.   He has had his redress in the only manner he knows.   I, therefore, request that no steps be taken against him.   I believe in him.   I will love him and win him by love."

When Barnardo was a medical student in East London, he was once involved in a riot in a beerhouse.   He had gone in to sell Bibles, but the drunken ruffians inside attacked him with fury, and finally flung him to the ground, grabbed the table, and placing it, legs upward, on his prostrate body, began to dance a tattoo. When the Bible seller was removed unconscious to his lodgings, he was bruised from head to foot, and had two broken ribs.   It was six weeks before he could move about again.   Not unnaturally, the police intervened and Barnardo was pressed to prosecute the ring-leaders. He refused. "I have begun with the Gospel," he said, "and I am determined not to end with the law."

Sir Frederick Treves has given to the world a yet more magnificent instance in "The Lamp Murder Case." [1] He has told in his own vivid prose the terrible story of the poor seamstress murdered by the drunken bestial fiend whom she had been misfortunate enough to marry. Having worked for her ailing daughter and this vicious loafer for years, she suffered death at his hands when, in a drunken quarrelsome fit, he flung two lighted lamps at her in the odorous Whitechapel slum where they lived. Her poor, burned body was carried into the London Hospital, and in the presence of the police and a magistrate her dying depositions were immediately taken. "Her face was hideously disfigured, the eyes closed, the lips swollen and bladderlike, and the cheeks charred in patches to a shiny brown. All her hair was burned off and was represented by a little greasy ash on the pillow, her eyebrows were streaks of black, while her eyelashes were marked by a line of charcoal at the edge of the lids. She might have been burned at the stake at Smithfield."

The doctor told her gently that she was dying. The magistrate warned her of the importance of her evidence. At the foot of the bed the police held up the blubbering beast who had murdered her. Then the swollen lips moved. "It was a pure accident," she said. She never spoke again. She died, as Desdemona

[1] *The Elephant Man, Etc.*, Treves, p. 104.

77

died, with a lie upon her lips. The Lord Christ understood. He, too, had looked down upon his murderers and stained the truth at love's demand. He said, "They know not what they do."

But perhaps no instance of sublime forgiveness comes quite so near the spirit of Calvary as that of Edmund Campion the English Jesuit. Finest of all the followers of Loyola who suffered for their faith in England, he has been praised by Protestants and Roman Catholics alike. In the days when his co-religionists were persecuted in this country, he perilously moved from place to place, nourishing their spiritual life, and narrowly avoiding arrest. But he was caught at last. Betrayed by one of his own people turned apostate, he was thrown into the Tower of London and thrice tortured on the rack. But nothing could shake either his constancy or serenity, and he heard his sentence to be hanged, drawn, and quartered at Tyburn, with the calmness of a man whose whole life was stayed on God. He actually broke into the Te Deum.

A day or two before his execution he had an amazing visitor. The spy who had betrayed him, and who knew his own life to be in hourly peril from the rage of old friends who had learned of his part in the arrest, staggered into Campion's cell, behind a jailer, and begged to be forgiven. The condemned man was weak from torture, and anticipating Tyburn, but he did not hesitate. He fully and freely forgave him. Still the traitor lingered. Would the gracious father do more? Would he help him escape from the fury of his pursuers? Even this the betrayed man was ready to do. Without a word of rebuke, he promised him a letter of introduction to a German nobleman who would accept his service, and on a rainy December morning he was tied to a hurdle and dragged from the Tower to Tyburn, through the filth and garbage of the London gutters. No hate, no bitterness, no lust for revenge. He went up the cart at the place of execution as though he were going to a wedding. In that last dread hour, poise and equanimity marked all that he did, and they were the fine fruit of his faith, his clear conscience, and his magnanimous forgiveness.

In the light of such evidence—only a tiny scrap of all which has been gathered—it ceases to be an open question whether or not revenge can be overcome. Christ is able to work the sweetest alchemy known among men. He can transform hate into love!

There remains a final question. Is forgiveness effective? Allowing that it is possible and healthy, what is the effect on the one forgiven? Some people fear that the effect is harmful. Merely to forgive, they argue, is to divorce crime from the consequences of crime, and encourage the criminal to act with impunity. Punishment, they say, is a necessary pillar to the edifice of the moral life, and simple forgiveness is dangerous in that it does not deter people from doing wrong.

It must be borne in mind that punishment and revenge are not synonymous, if only because, in revenge, a man insists on being the judge in his own quarrel, but it is still not hard to understand the view that is here expressed. Our sense of justice demands some redress, and we are not really satisfied that every sin brings its most awful punishment in some inescapable injury to the sinner's spiritual life.

Moreover, most of us have known instances of some great act of forgiveness which did not beget any moral response. In such an hour, when a valiant appeal to the highest fails, those who are not disciplined in disappointment and invincible in hope are tempted to abandon constraint and bludgeon their way into the evil wills of men. But Christ fought that fight in Gethsemane. He could have summoned twelve legions of angels, and he would not. He could have blasted his enemies with a word, but he suffered them to spit upon him and transfix him with great nails. When, on the day of the crucifixion, deep. darkness was over all the earth and the sun set in blood, it seemed as though love, and magnanimity, and truth, were on the scaffold yet again, and wrong filled the throne.

If the Cross of Christ could not break the stony hearts of some men, it should not surprise us if our lesser acts of forgiveness and restraint should have no immediate result in repentance. Let it be admitted freely that, within the limits of an individual life and as far as our own observation goes, forgiveness does sometimes appear to fail. But then it often succeeds! Hate *never* succeeds, except in producing hate. The history of the blood-feud proves that. The passion for revenge is sterile of all things good, but it is fecund in evil. After the first planting, revenge never needs planting again: it seeds itself. Only forgiveness can destroy the terrible weed. Forgiveness does not *always* succeed, but nothing else approaches

WHEN REVENGE MY HEART INVADES

success. It is impossible to stamp out enmity by hate. When the conqueror's foot is on the neck of his victim, the heart is still unsubdued. Revenge is patient. It will wait, and wait, and wait . . . and some day spring.

When Narvaez, the Spanish patriot, lay dying, his father-confessor asked him if he had forgiven all his enemies. Narvaez looked astonished and said, "Father, I have no enemies, I have shot them all." He thought he had. It was a vain hope. Only his death cheated them. Forgiveness alone destroys enemies. Jesus knew that. That is why his Cross towers above all the selfish competition of our modern life, ugly and holy, crude and sublime, coarse and serene; it symbolizes the single way by which hate can be overcome.

Nor is there any lack of evidence that forgiveness is often effective in the way which the Christian desires most. If it fails to affect the one forgiven, it is often fruitful in influence on those who look on.

Within a year of his attack on Gandhi, the murderous Moslem, whom the Mahatma so generously forgave, had been converted to Gandhi's cause. Barnardo always believed that his refusal to prosecute the brutes who assaulted him was a great help in his subsequent work. He said: "I believe this incident gave me a greater influence over the rough lads and girls of that quarter than I could have attained had I been preaching or teaching among them for years." [2] Campion's sublime act of forgiveness of the man who betrayed him led to the conversion of his jailer who was present at the interview.[3]

[2] *Dr. Barnardo*, Bready, p. 67.
[3] *Edmund Campion*, Simpson, pp. 443 f.

When Molly Ellis was kidnaped in Kohat in April, 1923, and snatched away by the same treacherous hands which had murdered her mother, all the world shuddered with horror and a punitive campaign was discussed. But the soldiers never marched. The girl was rescued by an unarmed Englishwoman who pierced those iron hills and brought her back in safety again. How came this woman to have such power? In this way. She was a nurse and married to a missionary doctor. One night, years before, her husband was called to the door by somebody begging for help and was stabbed to the heart in his own porch by one of the people he had served so well. So Mrs. Starr was widowed within two years of her marriage, but the only revenge she took on the murderers of her husband was to go on nursing them still. That was all. She went on nursing them still. The Afridis live for vengeance, and maintain their blood-feuds for generations, but service so sublime as this clutched even at their hard hearts. Her power among them could not be denied. Sir John Maffey, the Chief Commissioner of the District, said that she made a mark upon them better than all the drums and tramplings of an army corps. It was the fine fruit of forgiveness. What if it does sometimes fail? A doctor does not cease to be a respected physician because his remedy does not always cure. Forgiveness is not to be waved aside as foolish if it fails to evoke response in *every* heart.

The Cross stands and holds wide appealing arms to all who thirst after revenge. It seems to say, "This is how Jesus dealt with hate." He held it to him, and quelled it in his mighty heart of love. The boomerang lost its spring because the venom which flew out in his murder did not fly back again in revenge. So he appeals to us still and, having caught the vision, we can do no other. We *must* forgive.

> "It is the way the Master went.
> Should not the servant tread it still?"

VIII

WHEN SLOTH WOULD FILCH MY ZEAL AWAY

THE Apostle Paul was fond of describing himself as a bondservant of Jesus Christ, and a bondservant was one who had no other ambition than to do his master's will. He did not divide the hours between time spent in work and time used for himself. He did not watch a dial and count the overtime. All the hours of all the days were given to his Lord.

Most modern Christians fall lamentably short of the Apostolic level in the thrift of time. Enjoying more leisure than most of their forbears dreamed of, they do not "fill the unforgiving minute with its sixty seconds' worth of distance run." We cannot say of them what Wordsworth said of King Alfred, "Ease from this noble miser of his time, no moment steals." They do not know what Charles Darwin knew so well—"the difference between ten minutes and a quarter of an hour." They claim to be consecrated and pleaded with Jesus to take their moments and their days, but they are poor stewards of one of their most precious possessions, time. The wide fields of service lie before them, but the path they tread is littered with lost opportunities and neglected tasks. When their conscience accuses them they are ready with an "alibi." Quite often they say, "I had no time!" No time! They had all the time there was.

An ingenious inventor, troubled by the carnage of the roads, has invented a device for reducing the number of motor accidents. Many of them occur, he believes, because of the fatigue of the drivers, and he has pondered long on the opinion of doctors that the first sign of fatigue is laxity in the grip of the steering wheel. He does not hold, as some do, that a loose grip is ideal in driving. This is the invention. He has a loud buzzer attached to the wheel, which can only be kept quiet by a firm grasp. Any looseness of grip sets the drone in motion and brings the nodding driver to keen consciousness again. One wishes that there was a similar device in the spiritual world, something that would keep sleepy Christians vigorous and rouse them to efforts when sloth would filch their zeal away. The fields of service are so broad. The kinds of service are so varied. The needs of men are so acute and urgent. It is hard to understand how consecrated people can be deaf to the clamant call and indifferent to the swift passage of unredeemed time. The sundial says, "Traveler, it is later than you think."

The word "service" has grown in dignity of recent years. It used to belong "below stairs." "Going into service" was a humble phrase indicating some modest sphere of domestic help. But the word has been minted afresh and shines with a new luster. Such movements as Rotary are glad to employ the word in their motto: "Service above self!" The Navy is not ashamed to be called the "Senior Service." Commerce employs the term freely and lifts itself above the level of mere money-making. A man who renders no service to the community feels some compulsion to apologize.

In the garden by the High Court in Lahore is a statue of the first Lord Lawrence. He is depicted in riding-

85

kit, boots and spurs, and an open shirt, holding in one hand a pen and in the other a sword. When the statue was first erected Lawrence's famous words were carved on the plinth: "Will you be ruled by the pen or the sword?" Many times the statue has been defaced because it was regarded as an insult to the Indian Nation, and it has provoked more than one political agitation, so the authorities have discreetly altered the inscription. Disregarding what the noble lord said, the words now read, "With the pen and the sword I *serve* you." The alteration of that inscription reveals a revolution in thought. Service is seen, not to be menial, but to be the only true dignity. It would almost seem that the great ones of this earth are coming to realize that the Greatest of all meant what he said: "I am among you as he that serveth."

Odd as it may sound to the rising generation the word "service" is not a really old term in Christian usage. It ought to have been. There is the highest New Testament warrant for its use, but, at certain periods in the history of the Church, salvation came to be thought of in a very individualistic way, and a person's responsibility was limited to saving his or her own soul. When the cry was raised fifty years ago, "Saved to serve," and the social responsibilities of Christians were stressed, it seemed something new and wonderful to the youth of that day and greatly inspired them. It is not new to the youth of today. If service is neglected it is because of sloth rather than ignorance. Indeed, many plunge into service before they *are* saved, and without a divine motive for their toil. In some instances it is a refuge from spiritual unrest. Perplexed as to the real purpose of life, and unsure of God, they fly to the service of their fellows as an escape from a disordered mind. In the conflict of creeds, and faced perhaps with personal moral problems, the weary heart is glad to leave uncertainties aside for something that is concrete and sure. So they feed the hungry, and clothe the naked, and comfort themselves by the thought that, whatever is right or wrong in this world, it cannot be wrong to serve. And, of course, such service is never wrong. The defect in motive is serious and may lead to the early abandonment of the task, but the service, as service, is royal. "Inasmuch as ye have done it unto one of the least of these my brethren, ye have done it unto me."

Nor can it be denied that while no man is saved by serving others, many have been *led* to salvation along this path. When Dr. R. F. Horton called the people of Hampstead into mission work at Kentish Town, he invited Hugh Price Hughes to start the venture off. And Hugh Price Hughes told them that they were not going to Kentish Town to save Kentish Town, but Kentish Town would save Hampstead. So it proved. The work demanded £1,000 a year, and two hundred workers, and did immense good to all who took part. Service has that beneficent reactionary effect. It should take precedence, in its claim on our leisure, of all pursuits of personal culture and delight. It comes before all art undertaken as a hobby. Gandhi has often been reproached for giving no place to art in his plans for the renaissance of India, and Rabindranath Tagore complains that the stress on fleshly service makes the reformer's policy gloomy and arid. Tagore said, "The idea of non-co-operation with its mighty volume of sound, does not *sing* to me, its congregated menace of negation shouts . . ." Gandhi answered: "When all about me are dying for want of food, the only occupation permissible for me is to feed the hungry. . . . I have found it impossible to soothe suffering with a song." So have we. Man does not live by bread alone—but then he cannot live without it. The needs of our bodies are not our chief needs, but they are basic and urgent. Opportunities for service compass man's body, mind, and soul, and Christ is the Great Example in every aspect of this activity. Saved to serve! The need is patent and clamant, but not many respond to it and, of these, only a few are wise in the thrift of time and systematic in its consecrated use. The defect appears to be more often in the will than in the power, for many who are clearly equipped for service are not engaged upon it. They seem built for speed and utility, but there is something wrong with the engine. They remind one of a tortoise. The tortoise is beautifully stream-lined, but the mechanism belies the shape. We need men and women who will add to their capacity, consecration, and really give the utmost to the Highest.

Let us consider how Christ deals with the sin of sloth and what are the marks of the service which he demands from his disciples.

Service must be *unselfish*. Difficult as it is to understand our own complex motives, it is not impossible to discover whether selfish desires are at the heart of our service. Are we pained if people do not notice or praise us? Does it deeply hurt if somebody else gets the credit for what we have done? Allowing that egotism and the desire for self-display have their place in us all, is it a subordinate place in our service or the main end of our endeavors?

So many people are willing to serve Christ when they can serve themselves as well. So many are anxious to do something "big" or "special," not because their consecration is profound, but because they have a restless spirit and because the task that lay nearest did not satisfy them. Many such people have turned to Albert Schweitzer for counsel, and his wise words on the subject repay thought:

"It was evident that they have been brought to their decisions by quite secondary considerations. Only a person who can find a value in every sort of activity and devote himself to each one with full consciousness of duty has the inward right to take as his object some extraordinary activity instead of that which falls naturally to his lot. Only a person who feels his preference to be a matter of course, not something out of the ordinary, and who has no thought of heroism, but just recognizes a duty undertaken with sober enthusiasm, is capable of becoming a spiritual adventurer such as the world needs. There are no heroes of action: only heroes of renunciation and suffering. Of such there are plenty. But few of them are known, and even these not to the crowd." [1]

Obedience is better than sacrifice. To look upon the Church of God merely as a means of displaying one's own gifts is a low view of the Church. We might well question the degree of our consecration if we set limits

[1] *Out of My Life and Thought*, Albert Schweitzer, p. 110. Henry Holt and Company, publishers.

to it and stipulate that we will serve only here or there, or in that capacity or this. To rise and sing after such reservations,

> "Take my life and I will be
> Ever, only, all for Thee,"

borders on the blasphemous. If it is to be his service, it must be where he appoints, and to the vast majority of his disciples the appointment is to humdrum ordinary tasks. The novelty can be introduced in the spirit in which it is undertaken. To long for the limelight and fret for notice is a very immature stage in the life of service and quite often leads to desertion when the notice is denied. Disciples must be above that. The worth of our work is spoiled when people suspect that we are just campaigning for ourselves, whatever compensation the self is seeking. *The Times* reported recently that while the Plymouth fire brigade was fighting an outbreak of fire in a Devonport shop they were assisted in the noble work of rescue by a large cat. Ignoring the smoke and flames the cat plunged three times into the burning premises and each time saved a mouse. But the philanthropy belonged only to the appearance. The mice did not long survive.

Service should be as *secretive* as possible. It will assist our efforts after humility if we are at pains to avoid praise. A little encouragement is helpful to all people, but much praise is debilitating to the spiritual life. One comes to depend upon it. It increases our sensitivity to criticism and makes us impatient of contrary opinions. Our attitude toward it should not be merely negative. It is not enough that it is our motive: we must be positive in our efforts to escape it. When Verdi's first opera was produced in Florence, he stood within the shadows at the theater and watched the face of Rossini, the master musician. He wanted the smile of Rossini, and not all the hullabalooing of the gallery could conpensate him in its absence. So should the Christian toil, as obscurely as the work will allow, and having an eye fixed on the face of his Lord, live independent of the praise or blame of men.

In the last years of his life the saintly Curé D'Ars tasted a little comfort. In winter, somebody slipped a foot warmer under the loose board in the confessional on which he rested his feet. He never knew who did it. He did not even know it had been done. The secret servant was content that the saint was warm. Doubtless the angels knew the name.

Service is sometimes *lowly*—though never really menial. It is humbling to our pride and an excellent spiritual discipline that it should be so. We follow the Lord who washed his disciples' feet.

With that memory in mind, it is not uninstructive to recall the customs associated with Maundy Thursday. On that day the Pope and many monarchs used to wash the feet of twelve poor men in imitation of our Lord's washing the feet of his disciples. But the custom did not survive! Even when the ritual was observed the full obligation was frequently avoided. Queen Elizabeth only performed the rite after the yeomen of the laundry had first washed the pauper's feet with warm water and sweet herbs! James II was the last king of England to respect the custom. William III passed it on to his almoner and since 1750 Maundy money has been substituted for personal service.

There is a not unnatural shrinking in human nature from lowly service. We need not deplore the decay of a mere custom, but we do plead that pride is disciplined by humble toil, and, in the light of our Lord's example, none can claim exemption on the ground of status alone. If the feet-washing was a sacrament, it was a sacrament of lowly *personal* service. "The gift without the giver is bare."

Service is sometimes *costly*, very costly. It takes toll of us in various ways. It takes its toll when we hear ourselves unjustly charged with ulterior motives, when those we have helped with pure intent discuss what we were "getting out of it" ourselves, and fling our kindness in our face. In such an hour it is hard to be poised and to go on serving.

It takes toll of us in other ways. The missionaries know all about it. Writing in the fever-laden swamps of the Gaboon, Schweitzer says:

"Anxiety, trouble, and sorrow have been allotted to me at times in such abundant measure that, had my nerves not been strong, I must have broken down under the weight. Heavy is the burden of fatigue and responsibility which has lain upon me without break for years. I have not much of my life for myself, not even the hours I should like to devote to my wife and child." [2]

Many, besides the missionaries, could say the same thing. Service is costly. A glance at the Cross should

[2] *Op. cit.*, p. 281.

convince us of that. There is a poor woman in the city of Leeds, well known to a friend of mine, who has a scar across her heart and will have it till she dies. These were the circumstances. A neighbor's child fell ill and she went in to help with the nursing. The sickness was finally diagnosed as diphtheria, but in compassion for the distracted mother she still continued to help. Unhappily, the contact with infection imperiled her own child who fell sick with diphtheria too. In the passing of time her neighbor's child got better, but . . . her own child died! There is no lack of those who say she was a fool . . . or worse. If she takes her eyes from the Cross she is not sure herself. The cost of consecration! The price we pay! They might well hesitate to enter this royal service who are not willing to face the Cross.

Finally, service must be *systematic*. There is so much nebulous good will in the world, so many people who mean well and want to help, but never reach method and efficiency in their service. Philip Guedala said of Barrie that you can hear "the cheerful clatter of the cans as he goes round with the milk of human kindness!" We make no plea for noise, but we do plead for system. The man who faces life, as so many do, with a willingness "to do a good turn when he can" is making no adequate response to the call of Christ or the need of men. He is like the unsystematic giver who has a keen memory for his occasional benefactions but forgets the months when he never rose to generosity at all: he always supposes himself to be far more liberal than he is. It is not dissimilar with the man who is willing to do "a good turn," but has no real mind and method in his service.

Assume that he does a score of "good turns" in a year: many of them are trivial, and all of them would probably have been done additionally by a man who was serious in his work for God.

Nor is it possible to accept the oft-repeated excuse of men that they have no time or gifts for service. The fields are so broad and the needs so varied that Christ has a commission for every one; a mind bent on finding a sphere would not be lacking long. Let any man take a wide survey of the areas of need, and contrast the time he spends on himself with the time spent in service and see if he can then remain unrebuked by the glance of Christ.

Think of the glorious possibilities of personal evangelism, the simple and sincere commendation of our Lord to others. There is no service so everlastingly profitable as this, or one more natural and necessary from all disciples.

If this task seems too ambitious for a reticent soul (though it ought not to be), think of the wide scope offered to any who would constrain people to the Christian fellowship. Samuel Chadwick had a man in his church at Stacksteads who was a genius in this lovely service. He says, "He developed a marvelous faculty for hunting big sinners out from the haunts of vice to the house of God . . . and was honored by the Holy Ghost in that kind of work above any man I know." [3] Any church is richer by such men and women. These cunning hunters are needed at every level of the social scale.

Think of the wide field offered by the Sunday school

[3] *Samuel Chadwick*, Dunning, p. 57.

and the many organizations for the young clubs, brigades, scouts, and guides. He who influences a child influences the future and puts posterity in his debt.

Consider the claims of the overseas missions with all their beneficent work of evangelism and teaching and healing. The missionary is in the very van of those who work for world peace and when his toil languishes it is not usually because his zeal abates but because the supporters at home have failed him.

Think of the orphanages and all their gracious care for neglected and homeless children. Think of the blind, the deaf and dumb, the malformed, and the crippled. Many people give an occasional thought, or a coin, or a visit, to these needy ones when the cause is pressed upon their notice, but it is systematic service alone that will really succor them.

Nor can one forget in these days of wide commercial depression the need of the unemployed. However limited one's financial resources may be, there is still scope for service among the victims of our economic errors. Respect, sympathy, and practical kindliness save human nature from collapse. The voluntary hospitals need organized help and the sick in home and infirmary are lifted up by cheerful visitation. A friend of mine retired from business in his fifties in order to give some of the best years of his life to social service. He retired to an opulent seaside resort, but found the opportunities there somewhat limited and moved back again to a densely populated area. He spends many hours of every week in the infirmaries. Not feeling equal to the kind of visitation some can do, he goes from

95

ward to ward with a portable gramophone and some excellent records and radiates good cheer. It is delightful to hear him start a competition, and offer a cigar to the old gentleman who knows the name of the piece of music he will play next. The inmates who have no visitors at all are all known to him and are the objects of his special care, and on their birthday some little inexpensive present comes to mark the anniversary. He is much loved. The authorities of the infirmaries grant him many privileges because his discretion is unfailing. He does not count himself a gifted man for service, but he is keen to do what he can. His inspiration is all drawn from his Lord.

Hospitality is another great form of service; not chiefly hospitality extended to folks we like, but held out generously to the lonely, or to young men and women who live in lodgings, and cannot ask us again. I know at least one great Church leader who was saved to God and the Church by the simple hospitality of kindly people when he was a lonely law student in a Scottish town.

Nor can we forget the ministry of letters. One has known invalids, as well as folks of strictly limited time, who have exercised glorious service with the pen. Writing often under the guidance of God and neither expecting nor desiring an answer to many of their letters, they have dispensed comfort and cheer, encouragement and hope, and done incalculable good. Often those letters arrive *just* when they are needed. I once endeavored to save a man convicted of murder from the gallows. Some doubt as to his guilt lingered in my mind and in the mind of others, but the attempt to gain a reprieve failed. On the day of the execution, when his distraught relatives were at my home and we were trying to make that terrible day bearable for them, two letters arrived by the same post. Both were anonymous. The first was as filthy an effusion as I have ever read: its mildest hope was that I might have been hung with the condemned man. The second was so sweet and healing that it might have come from heaven itself. I think it did.

How can men and women say that they have neither time nor gifts for service? In fields so broad, the busiest and the least gifted can find a task. The great cause of peace clamors for champions. Intemperance lifts its ugly head again. Cruelty to birds and animals demands denunciation. The gambling craze is extending its tentacles into every area of life. Discharged prisoners return to normal life every day and offer a wonderful opportunity to any who are invincible in hope.

> "The Son of God goes forth to war . . .
> Who follows in His train?"

IX

WHEN CHARITY ENDS AT HOME

PREACHERS often speak with great scorn against money. They seem to have received without qualification the Biblical dictum that the love of money is the root of all evil. It does not modify their scorn to remember that the Revisers softened the expression, and make Paul say, "The love of money is the root of all *kinds* of evil." To them, money is the villain of the piece, and they place the villain in the pillory again and again.

That they are stressing an aspect of the truth cannot be doubted, but it is foolish to regard the money as evil in itself. Granted a good will, money can be put to the most beneficent uses and, if it cannot buy happiness, it can often create the conditions of it.

George Gissing had been very poor himself and, in the *Private Papers of Henry Rycroft,* he protests vehemently against disparaging the power of money. He says:

"You tell me that money cannot buy the things most precious. Your commonplace proves that you have never known the lack of it. When I think of all the sorrow and the barrenness that has been wrought in my life by want of a few more pounds per annum that I was able to earn, I stand aghast at money's significance. What kindly joys have I lost, those simple forms of happiness to which every heart has a claim, because of poverty? Meetings with those I loved made impossible year after year; sadness and misunderstanding, nay, cruel alienation arising from inability to do the things I wished, and which I might have done had a little

98

money helped me; endless instances of homely pleasure and contentment curtailed, or forbidden, by narrow means. I have lost friends merely through the constraint of my position; friends I might have made have remained strangers to me; solitude of the bitter kind, the solitude that is enforced at times when heart and mind long for companionship often cursed my life, solely because I was poor." [1]

The recorder said recently at the Old Bailey, "A couple of pounds very often saves a life, and sometimes a soul."

Money as money is not evil. It speeds on errands of mercy and lends itself to a thousand philanthropies. It feeds the hungry, clothes the naked, and succors men who are tempted to suicide. It is the insensate *love* of riches which is the perilous thing.

If it were not so common, it would border on the incredible that men should allow their lives to be blighted by the greed of pelf. The disease is so deadly. It robs its victims of inner peace. Their very faces are stamped with an avaricious look and, in extreme cases, they walk about like a roaring lion seeking whom they may devour. Sweetness and serenity vanish from their nature. They become as metallic as the coin they seek.

That familiarity breeds contempt is a rule which admits of few exceptions, but one of those exceptions is money. Like some deadly diabetes of the soul, the thirst cannot be cured by drinking. The more the victim has the more he wants. In the pleasure of accumulation all lovely things perish. Friendship, culture, and spiritual sensitivity may each be sacrificed to this one ab-

---

[1] Published by E. P. Dutton and Company, Inc., New York.

sorbing passion. The possession or lack of money is taken as a valid test of other men, and a saint is waved aside contemptuously as "a-two-pound-ten-a-week man." When the condition becomes chronic, the money is valued for itself alone, and is not even thought of as a means to comfort or power. Some insane satisfaction is anticipated in the surprise men will feel when the newspaper announces that Mr. So-and-so died worth so many hundreds of thousands. And for a pleasure like this men will sacrifice the most precious things they have!

It reminds one of the epitaph:

"Here at Stoke-by-Nayland once lived a wealthy miser who pulled down crows' nests for fuel and got the usual reward of suchlike thrift in having half a million of money half a minute before he died, and nothing half a minute later."

I once went through the Mawddach valley which cradles Dolgelley in North Wales. It is one of the beauty spots of the world. The sharp black shoulder of Cader Idris rises bleak against the sky. The tree-muffled hills skirt the stream as the stream winds its sinuous way to the sea. At the estuary itself, the view is incomparably lovely. It is impossible to decide whether one loves it most when the tide is full and laps the craggy banks, or when it is low and reveals a hundred curling rivulets in the sand. But satiated travelers have thrilled again at this.

Yet the lovely valley is spoiled in one part. An ugly mine mars the view. It is disused now, but the earth lies torn and bleeding around its silent shaft. It was a gold mine—but it did not prove a commercial success. They spoiled this lovely valley for a gold mine—and it did not pay!

It is a parable. It never does pay to spoil the beauty of character by the love of gold. Money is only a "thing." Not all the gold in the world is worth one soul. "What shall it profit a man if . . . ?"

Nor must it be forgotten that the peril of riches does not depend on their *possession*. The inordinate longing for them is the deadly thing. A man is in the grip of money whose little hoard would be entirely beneath the notice of a serious financier, if that man puts pre-eminent worth upon money, and lives and longs for nothing else.

Who can deliver us from this lust of wealth for which women have lost their virtue, and men their character and name? Christ can deliver us. He is able! He was sold himself for thirty pieces of silver, so he knows what men will do for lucre. Yet, without money and without price, he summons to himself all who live in the grip of mammon, and will save to the uttermost those who come unto God by him.

Nor is the method of his salvation obscure. He teaches mastery of money by fidelity in stewardship. He would have his followers look upon *all* their resources as held in trust for God. Time, talents, home, books, position . . . and money with the rest. Consequently, there is no easy rule to be applied, without distinction, to all incomes. Useful as many people have found the maxim to give a tenth to God, it is not an adequate solution of the problem. A tenth would be too much for some, and far too little for others. It encourages also the false idea that nine-tenths are so entirely ours that one can do what one likes with them without any reference to God.

Jesus would have us look upon all we possess as God's and then, however absurd it may seem to some people, there cease to be any real problems of finance, but only problems of guidance. What would God have us do? If my income permits it, shall I cease to work in paid employment and give my whole time to some God-directed service? Or shall I continue to earn that I may have more to give? Or am I of those few who, without any recognizable source of income, are called to whole time and unpaid service, and who must depend directly on God for the sustenance of every day?

And that brings us to the most dangerous thing about money. It seduces the heart from God, and men look upon it as the ground of their security and the spring of their confidence. When some dark fear of the future crosses their mind, their thoughts dart off to their money instead of to their God. "I will be all right," they think. "I've got that." Yet that simple movement of the mind has perilous consequences. In the passing of the years it builds a false faith on something which cannot sustain them in the darkest hours of life and filches trust from the One who is alone sufficient for their need. Anything which weakens the conviction that our security is only in God is dangerous, and nothing weakens that conviction more than the love of money. A high sense of stewardship is the antidote. Those who possess it could bear even to hear what our Lord said to the Rich Young Ruler and not turn sorrowfully away.

Faithfulness in stewardship has another glorious fruit too. It saves a man from cursing his children with a fortune. It is serious enough, in all conscience, to live for money and go to face the Great Audit with a record of jealous hoarding and niggardly giving, but it is not less serious to pass on the awful responsibility to a child. What splendid lives have been spoiled in this way. How few can carry the responsibility well. Of what fine service has the world been robbed in those who never needed to extend themselves because their fathers made them "independent," and who never displayed their best because they never faced the provocation of awkward circumstances. If a child is fit and educated, he only needs a start. The byways of biography are littered with the slight and inept records of the sons of wealthy men. Wesley foresaw this awful danger among the men who followed him, and with his customary plainness of speech he warned them against the peril of leaving fortunes to their children. Though he was childless himself his own use of money was plainer than his words. He made tens of thousands of pounds out of his publications, and died leaving a couple of silver spoons.

Nor do the gains of stewardship end even here. Knowing both the worth and worthlessness of money, and knowing also how ridiculous is its claim to be the chief aim of life, the steward can never fawn on wealth in others. It amazes and saddens him to see the strange adulation which men offer to other men merely because they possess much money, and he gazes in bewilderment on a world where values are so strangely mixed that money is pressed on pugilists and those who amuse us, and denied to poets, and master musicians, and men engaged in medical research. Milton received £5 for *Paradise Lost*, and another £5 when the first edition was exhausted: £10 in all for the greatest work of the second greatest figure in English letters. Tunney received $200,000 for his first fight with Dempsey. Beethoven lost £20 in producing the immortal Ninth Symphony, and Sir Donald Ross, who discovered the secret of malaria, had to sell his papers in the eventide of life to provide himself and his wife with modest comfort; but a star baseball player earns (or receives) $30,000 a year for knocking a ball with a bat. There are fortunes for fisticuffs, but poverty for poetry and research. Yet, with all these absurd examples before their eyes, men still fawn upon wealth, and treat its possession as a ground for praise. Not so, the steward. He cannot despise money because he knows the precious things that it can do, but he cannot praise it. It is a "thing"; it is meant to serve life. He holds it lightly, but uses it wisely and generously, and always as God directs.

So God prepares his servants for the Final Audit. The steward knows that at his best he is an unprofitable servant, but he waits quietly on God for guidance, and seeks to use his substance in accordance with the Divine will. At the last he hopes to hear his Master say, "Well done, good and faithful servant, enter thou into the joy of thy Lord."

Nor is it hard to cite instances of devoted stewards, to some of whom the most challenging guidance came, but who replied to an unusual word with a swifter response and happier heart than the Rich Young Ruler could command. At least twice in his ministry George Augustus Selwyn, the pioneer Bishop of New Zealand, voluntarily faced life for extended periods "without visible means of support." For years Dr. John Clifford ministered to his people, living on a modest sum and resisting all the tempting offers of wealthier Churches, covering the country at the call of hard-pressed men and declining any remuneration other than his third-class fare, and opening his lean purse to the needy again and again. When on his day of life the night was falling, generous friends bought him an annuity, and thanked God for the privilege of being permitted to help so true a prophet.

Fenton Hall, one of the pioneer missionaries to Amazonia, felt it right to give all he had to God when he gave himself. When he left the Royal Air Force, he had £1,000. He gave £700 to the World Evangelization Crusade and £300 to the Missionary College of the same movement. He made no rules for other people, but he was certain it was right for him. Then he said, with a sigh of relief, "I am glad to think that I am now free to put my whole trust in God."

Kagawa of Japan lives in a Japanese slum on a dollar and a half a month, and uses the rest of his money on the poor and suffering around him.

C. T. Studd inherited a portion of his father's fortune

when he was twenty-five. He had calmly decided two years previously what he would do with it. When the news reached him in China, his inheritance, so far as he could judge, was £29,000, but to allow for a margin of error, he decided to start by giving £25,000. One memorable day, January 13, 1887, he sent off four checks of £5,000 each, and five of £1,000. He sent £5,000 to Mr. Moody, £5,000 to Mr. George Muller of Bristol, £5,000 to Mr. George Holland in Whitechapel, and £5,000 to Commissioner Booth Tucker of the Salvation Army. To Miss McPherson, Miss Ellen Smyly, General Booth, the Rev. Archibald Brown, and Dr. Barnardo he sent £1,000 each. Each gift was directed to some deserving work. Later, he discovered that he still had a balance in hand and he divided it between the China Inland Mission and the Salvation Army. When he married he was a poor man.[1]

Of course, it was all very imprudent. Every scrap of worldly wisdom rises in us to condemn the course he took. But were Apostles ever prudent? And can it be denied that for the forty-one years of his married life God cared for this man, and his wife and children, and the work to which they had given their hands?

In days when meanness infects men and women even in the Church of God, and generous impulses are often throttled before they can find expression in deeds; when economy is preached like a gospel, and practiced first on charities; when every excuse is seized upon by the niggardly to cover their greed; when men who should know

[1] *C. T. Studd*, N. P. Grubb, p. 66.

better die and leave large fortunes over which others not seldom quarrel; when noble enterprises languish for lack of means, and hospitals remain unbuilt, and orphan children uncared for; when missionaries are recalled, and the wheels of God's endeavor turn more slowly because his children suppose themselves to be possessors when they are only stewards . . . then it is a good thing that striking instances of sacrificial giving should be thrust upon our notice, and our meanness rebuked by men who gave till they could give no more.

I do not know that any of these men would have insisted that others should do precisely what they did. They just felt that it was right *for them,* and only Eternity will reveal all the generosity that their sacrifice has inspired. They would, however, insist that all men and women are but stewards of their entire possessions, and should use them with strict concern for the will of their true Owner. They covet for their fellows the joy of working miracles with money. What happiness can the mean know which is comparable with the joy of the generous? To have a share in the beneficent work of missions—medical, educational, and evangelical; to succor the orphan or neglected child; to bring the light of hope to the blind, and lend an arm to the halt and maimed; to foster medical research, or aid the voluntary hospitals; to bring sweetness in slumdom, and a breath of sea air to the sick; to help the unemployed to help themselves; to give the promising children of poverty a start in life; to make the eventide bright for the aged poor.

What scope for joy! What opportunities to make the

angels talk! What golden chances of quietly winning love! To think that a man should miss this dear delight and compensate himself by looking at a passbook.

Thou fool! Some night your soul shall be required of you, and then you will find that you only have what you have given away.

X

WHEN JEALOUS THOUGHTS INVADE MY HEART

THE word "jealousy" is used in the Bible in two senses. Its teaching upon this topic cannot be understood unless this distinction is kept clearly in mind. The Bible knows a good jealousy and a bad jealousy, and it is a pity that we are obliged to use the same word for both attitudes of heart. As instances of the good jealousy one may cite the words, "For I the Lord thy God am a jealous God," or the pathetic moan of Elijah at Horeb, "I have been jealous for the Lord God of Hosts," or the cry of Zechariah, "I am jealous for Jerusalem and for Zion with a great jealousy," or the plea of the Apostle Paul to the fickle Corinthians, "Would to God you would bear with me a little . . . for I am jealous over you with a godly jealousy." All these are instances of a good jealousy. They are expressions of the zeal of love. They find their force not in a passion for self but in a great passion for the beloved.

It was because God loved his people with a full abounding love that he was jealous for them. He was not jealous for himself, nor crudely insistent on his mead of respect and praise, but jealous for their highest good. What utterly lost and undone creatures we should be if his love brooked any rival in our hearts. "I the Lord thy God am a jealous God." It was because Elijah was full of consuming love for God and his nation that he could say, "I have been jealous for the Lord God of hosts!" There is no self-love here. He was entirely regardless of his own fortunes and courted death to extol his God. Nor was it different with Paul. Throughout the eleventh chapter of his second epistle to the Corinthians he labors to prove how disinterested his service for them had been. He is jealous—he cannot deny it—but it is a godly jealousy. He wanted no glory in being their evangelist, but his love toward them gave him no peace until they had entered into all the fullness of Christ. For this kind of jealousy we have nothing but wonder, love, and praise. It is devotion at white heat. It gives its all, and finds its all in giving. It is a passion worthy of the heart of God.

But this is not "jealousy" in the sense in which the word is commonly used. This is as hateful as the other is praiseworthy, and as foul and poisonous as the other was cleansing and pure. It is envy born of some deep love of self.[1]

It was that feeling of coldness and resentment that stirred in your heart when you heard somebody else praised, somebody with whom you had matched yourself in thought and to whom you fancied yourself superior. It was that dislike which nearly turned to bitterness when they attracted more attention than you attracted, or sipped the waters of success a little deeper, or took a position you had marked as your own. All these were the stirrings of jealousy. It was jealousy that took the heart out of the congratulations you felt obliged to give; that kept you silent when you heard them unfair-

[1] Of the relation of jealousy and envy, cf. *Social Psychology*, McDougall, pp. 136-139.

ly criticized; that made you secretly glad when they stumbled and fell. It was jealousy, petty, loathsome jealousy, the jealousy which, at its worst, can be incredibly cruel.

Look for a moment at the peculiarities of this vice. It is not normally directed against those who might seem most to provoke it, the people who so far outsoar us in attainment as almost to move in another world. It is focused on someone in our immediate circle and who, in point of achievement, only just outstrips our best, someone seeking applause from the same company of people. The provincial singers are not jealous of Robeson or Chaliapin, of Galli-Curci or Tetrazzini. They modestly allow that such singing is vastly superior to their own, and yet they are not jealous of them. It is rather of someone whom they commonly meet and with whom they have matched themselves in thought; someone whose attainment others believe to be just above their own (though they are convinced that it is definitely below it); it is of this one that they feel the stirring of jealousy and the envy born of deep self-love.

This significant fact can be further confirmed by observing the workings of this vice in a business house. Office boys are not normally consumed with jealousy of the manager, or junior clerks of the directorate. These senior officials are usually accepted as part of the constitution of things, and if there is any mental comparison with them in the juvenile mind it is only a healthy provocation to keener effort as they visualize what they may become. Jealousy does not usually fill up a gulf: it gets into a crack. It is of colleagues and those who share our status while they surpass us in prowess of whom we are tempted to jealousy: the equals who prove themselves more than equals and are selected for certain favors, and gratified with coveted praise. The people who are doing the same thing that we are doing but doing it better. If we are to be proof against this invidious vice, it is imperative that we learn to appreciate those who *just* surpass us in our own calling, for jealousy feeds on fine distinctions and seldom crosses the professional line. The Latin proverb says: "The potter is envious of the potter, the smith of the smith."

Another peculiarity of jealousy may be noted here. Our friends and relations are not secure against its poisoned fang. There is a widespread cynical maxim that the good fortune of our friends makes us envious and, while it is not always true, it is true often enough to give the phrase wide currency. It explains moreover why the apostle's counsel, "Weep with those that weep," has begotten a much greater response than his complementary word, "Rejoice with those that rejoice." A score follow the first injunction for everyone who heeds the second. The former does not provoke us to envy: the latter does. It takes a magnanimous spirit to see an old associate, whose circumstances have been cast in the same mold as our own, and with whom we have traveled on equal terms for years, shoot ahead and leave us lumbering in the same old ruts. It puts a strain on friendship, and often the barrier is not in the man who succeeds but in the one who is left behind. He may take a sour view of his friend's success and hint that it was achieved in unworthy ways, and their friendship withers because of jealousy.

Let us suspect ourselves when we begin to sneer at other people's success. When we imply that the business man's progress was probably the result of sharp practice, or the public speaker's gifts rather flashy and superficial things with no solid merit beneath them, or the beautiful girl, who has excited our envy, not so beautiful in character and disposition as her face would imply. It is hard to tell the truth about people we do not like and almost impossible when we envy them. Our little innuendoes and tainted hints will not deceive other people, for they will see the envy in our soul, but they deceive ourselves. Prejudice impairs our judgment and poisons our feeling, and peace and happiness fade out of our life.

And if envy often spoils friendship, what havoc it has been known to create in the branches of a family. The democracy of home and the glorious equality we shared when we played at the same hearth as children together is often altered by the world. One brother succeeds; another will hew wood and draw water till he dies. A touch of patronage on one side and a bit of envy on the other and the old fellowship has gone. Somehow it seems to foster our sense of inferiority when one in the family circle, begotten of the same parents and enjoying no greater advantages than we had ourselves, wins through to conspicuous success. No loophole seems left for the grudging spirit that would explain the triumph away on other grounds, and it seems to force us to face some inferiority in ourselves. Should the envy be nurtured by any jealousy between their wives, the gulf becomes deep indeed. Oscar Wilde used to tell a fable which will partly illustrate the point. The Devil was once crossing the Libyan Desert when he came upon a group of small fiends who were tempting a holy hermit. They tried him with the seductions of the flesh; they sought to sow his mind with doubts and fears; they told him that all his austerities were nothing worth. But it was all of no avail. The holy man was impeccable. Then the Devil stepped forward. Addressing the imps he said, "Your methods are too crude. Permit me for one moment. This is what I should recommend." Going up to the hermit he said, "Have you heard the news? Your brother has been made Bishop of Alexandria." The fable says: "A scowl of malignant jealousy clouded the serene face of the holy man."

We do not say that this is typical, but we do say that it is not uncommon. Many families are honeycombed with jealousy. What a boon if jealousy could be mastered? What a sweetening of so many areas of life? This is a foul thing which poisons the professions and makes a rent in the fabric of friendship and family life. It turns up in a dozen different disguises and infects every level of society. Famous men have often been guilty of it, struggling for supremacy in the public esteem which held them equal. In the early eighteenth century Richardson and Fielding were the two most popular of English novelists. Fielding said that Richardson was a "solemn prig," and Richardson affirmed that Fielding was "a low and vulgar fellow." Artists are not exempt. There was quite a feud at one time between Millais and G. M. Ward. When Millais in 1852 exhibited his "Ophelia," Ward said to him,

"What do you call this thing?"

"I call it 'Ophelia,' " said Millais.

"Hem! I call it 'Oh Failure,' " said Ward, and he walked on.

Most sad of all are the personal jealousies of ecclesiastics. Even to old age the antipathy between Manning and Newman was acute. "I hear you have been to Birmingham," said Manning to Wilfrid Ward, "to visit Cardinal Newman. Shall I tell you, Wilfrid Ward, what has ruined that man's career? One thing and one thing only: Temper! Temper!! *Temper!!!*"

Who can cure this evil thing? How shall jealousy be done away? Who is able?

Christ is able! He can uproot this rank weed in human hearts and plant the lovely flower of magnanimity in its place. Many there are who can testify to his power. Jealousy consumed them. All their views of life were jaundiced and bitter. Then Jesus came and took control and worked a blessed transformation.

First, he adjusted the habit of making comparisons. The wrong direction of this tendency is the root of envy. It begins in a wrong comparison. We compare ourselves with our fellows and not with our Lord. To compare oneself with Jesus is a healthy spiritual discipline much practiced by the saints. It humbles the heart, condemns sin in every form, and imparts a great passion after holiness. To practice comparison with one's fellows is often to be trapped into sin. If they are not as virtuous as we are, we slip into spiritual pride; if they are more virtuous than we are, we are tempted to imply that it is only appearance and they are possibly hypocrites; if they have tasted more of the sweetness of success than we have done, we often slide into envy. The impulse to comparison must be redirected. Focus it on Jesus. Practice comparison with him and good will come of it, but to practice comparison with our more fortunate fellows is the direct road to jealousy.

A small boy once worried his mother for a penknife and at last his importunity wore down her opposition and she bought him one. He was happy just for an hour. He went next door to show the penknife to his friend and came back miserable, and when his mother chided him for ingratitude, he said, "Jim has a penknife also. But his penknife has three blades and mine only has two." How foolish it is to lose the pleasure of the things we have by dwelling on the slight advantages of our neighbor. But it is not a fault confined to children. It is the daily error of half the world and in our folly we let the spirit of envy filch our happiness away.

Quite half of our jealousy is born in ignorance. If we knew the toil that success requires, and the disappointments of it sometimes, and the hidden sorrows of some that we envied, we should be ashamed of our jealousy. We judge by the surface of their life; we often do not know what lies beneath. Years ago Mr. A. G. Gardiner wrote a little essay on Sir John Simon and spoke at length of his great and unqualified success. He described him as prancing down a rose-strewn path to a shining goal. He thought that success in such a measure as Sir John had enjoyed it must rob life of much of its adventurous delight. And then Mr. Gardiner remembered something else and he added in parenthesis, "I speak here only of his *public* career: in his private life he has known the bitterest sorrows." Many of us forget the parenthesis. We see simply the surface of our neighbor's life and know nothing of his secret sorrows. Yet, even if there were no secret sorrows at all and God in his wisdom had appointed a path of blazing sunshine to someone else, that does not release us from our discipleship or give us ground for jealousy. He is the rightful Lord of all life. "It is he that hath made us and not we ourselves."

Let us keep our eyes fixed on Jesus and satisfy this impulse to comparison in a way that will yield a spiritual gain.

Another way in which Jesus rids the heart of envy is to enlarge the gamut of our prayers. Prayer can be a great purge. It is not possible to pose to Jesus and hide from him the envy that we feel, but if we confess our sin he will teach us how to turn envy into good will.

When Dr. F. B. Meyer first went to the Northfield Convention, he attracted great crowds. People poured in to hear his popular addresses, and for some years no speaker was more welcome than he. But in the passing of time Dr. Campbell Morgan came to Northfield and the crowd left Meyer to attend the Bible studies of his brilliant colleague, and to more than one person Meyer confessed that he found himself liable to jealousy. "The only way I can conquer my feeling," he said, "is to pray for him daily, which I do." That is how the saints deal with this evil growth when they discover, with an awful shock of surprise, that it has taken root in their consecrated heart. But their prayers give Jesus the opportunity he is seeking and he plucks it out.

Nor can any other speak the same healing, remedial words that he commands. What balm it is to a poor, frustrated, neglected, ignored, and impotent soul to be assured from Heaven that his gifts and service, however lightly regarded on earth, are not less precious to God than those of his most brilliant contemporary. No man remains envious who really sets his whole heart on the approval of heaven because that secures an independence of the praise and blame of earth. The simplest servant of the kingdom, quietly confident that he is doing his best, may feel the smile of God upon him. There is no richer reward in store for anyone. All the plaudits of all the people cannot really compensate for its absence. Being sure of God's approval no man need envy the praise of earth.

"The Master praise; what are men?"

And when Christ does rule in a heart what marvels of magnanimity he can effect. Henry Melvill Gwatkin was lecturer in ecclesiastical history at Cambridge in 1884 when it was decided to endow a chair in that subject. Most of his friends were confident that Gwatkin would be appointed and he was strong in hope himself. But when the decision was made the choice fell upon Mandell Creighton, who was then Vicar of Embleton in Northumberland, and the keenness of Gwatkin's disappointment can be imagined. He had been doing the work for twelve years. It would not have been surprising if some bitterness had crept into his heart when he heard that the honor had gone to another. But next day he wrote to Creighton, and his letter is a glorious example of the Christian's triumph over jealousy. He said:

"For myself I am ready to work under you and to support you loyally in all that falls to me to do. So far as I know my own heart, no jealousy of yesterday shall ever rise on my side to mar the harmony and friendship in which I ask and hope to live with the first Professor of Ecclesiastical History in Cambridge." [2]

When he succeeded Creighton in the chair in 1891, the promise of his letter had been kept in spirit and in truth.

[2] *Life and Letters of Mandell Creighton*, L. Creighton, Vol. I, p. 245.

XI

WHEN SIN CONTRIVES TO CLOAK ITSELF

THE first time that Paul is mentioned in the New Testament is in connection with a judicial murder. He is the greatest figure in the early church after Jesus, but when the curtain rises on his career, he is implicated in a crime. Stephen had defended himself before the Sanhedrin with great skill (and with great scorn), and they rushed upon him in blind fury and dragged him out of the city to stone him to death. It was a form of execution nearly as terrible as crucifixion. Flung against the city wall, his murderers picked up stones and hurled them at him, pounding him to death. He passed out magnificently. The first martyr was worthy of his pre-eminence. As the cruel stones struck him, on his limbs, on his body, on his head, he struggled to rise and then knelt down. Lifting up his voice, he cried, "Lord, lay not this sin to their charge" . . . and died.

And Paul was there. He had taken no part in the murder. He had thrown no stone. No bleeding wound on the martyr's body could be put down to him—but he had been looking after their coats! He had been an accessory both before and after the fact. He had consented to it, and was therefore implicated in it. He had encouraged them in evil, and lent his support to their foul crime. Though he might have left the scene of the murder saying, "I never did it," a smear of the martyr's blood was on his hands.

Now that is a mode of sin, not regarded with sufficient seriousness, but evil in the extreme. There are murderers who never touched the poison, drew the pistol, or used the knife. There are thieves who never picked a pocket, picked a lock, or sacked a safe. There are people who stir up strife without ever appearing in a quarrel themselves. There are moral lepers who have never visited a house of ill fame. They are behind the scenes, looking after the coats, dropping a poisoned hint or an inflammatory word. You may not guess their power, but it is sinister, corrosive, and deadly. People who commit crimes are often colorless personalities, and may be in no sense hardened in sin. They may have come under a powerful influence and be the cat's-paw of someone else. If you want to know the real genesis of the trouble you may need to look behind and ask: "Who dropped the hint, who sowed the idea, who nurtured the foul thought, and who minded the coats?"

One of the last women to be hanged in England was hanged in those very circumstances because the law says, and says rightly, that the one who inspires the crime is as guilty as the one who does it. Mrs. Thompson did not murder her husband. She was walking home with him from Ilford Station on the night of October 4, 1922, after a visit to a theater, when a young man leaped out of the shadows and stabbed her husband to death at her side. *She* did not murder him. Indeed, she screamed out for help at once, and the first people to arrive found her convulsed in horror and fear.

But when the trial was finished she was hanged as well as the murderer. Telltale letters were found in his possession, letters from her, letters which told of her hate for her husband and recommending her correspondent to read novels concerning "the eternal triangle," and especially those in which the situation was solved by the death of the third party. The murderer was but a boy of twenty. The woman was eight years his senior and stronger in influence. She had not done the murder, but the law said that she must die.

The Judicial Committee of the Privy Council was engaged with a not dissimilar case a short time ago. They were asked to reverse a decision of the Supreme Court of Hong Kong which had convicted a certain Chinaman to death for procuring a murder. He had not committed the crime himself, but he had dropped a hint to his chauffeur, and his chauffeur had dropped a hint to an assassin, and the assassin had done the deed. And when the thread of evidence was unwound, the Supreme Court of Hong Kong said, "*You* inspired this murder and you must die," and when the judgment was challenged before the Privy Council in London, the Privy Councilors said that it was right.

Behind every evil deed there is a thought, an influence. The thought does not always belong to the same mind to which the hand belongs. There are men and women who are received in all walks of society, and held in high respect, whose influence is evil because they are pulling the strings of sin.

I said to a man once, in my efforts to patch up a quarrel in slumdom, "I hope that you had nothing to do with causing the dispute," and he looked both hurt and indignant. He said, "What had I got to do with it? I wasn't even there. It's true I met him a day or two before and . . . I did just say . . . 'If I were you, I'd give him one on the nose' . . . but I hadn't anything to do with it."

Have you ever had a part in a quarrel in a slightly more refined way than that? Have you fed a person's anger? Have you kept in the background yourself, but whispered in his ear, "Get your own back. Be even with him. Wait till you get your chance and then let him have it." Have you spoken like that? Then you share the guilt as well.

There would be far fewer thieves if there were fewer receivers; if, in the background, there were no un-scrupulous rascals living on the burglar's pluck and the burglar's vice; tossing the thief himself a mere pittance as the price of his peril, and taking the major share of the profits themselves. If there were no such sinister figures behind the scenes of our social life, the number of thieves would be drastically reduced. And there would be far fewer quarrels if there were no fomenters of quarrels, no people who foster another's hate by whispered words and poisoned thoughts. What need there is to pit our strength against all that is evil, and be swift in conversation to set any action in as kind a light as it will bear. Jesus is expert in convincing us that no word of resentment must be fostered and that the value and necessity of forgiveness must be stressed. He said, "Blessed are the peacemakers: for they shall be called the children of God."

Or, perhaps, it was not a quarrel that you were im-plicated in. You may not be a conductor of hateful influences at all, but . . . have you been a conductor of bawdy stories? Has any word of yours inflamed the lusts of some young life and made it harder for that man or woman to be pure?

A clergyman told me once that when he was a boy a man repeated some foul stories to him and hung upon the walls of his mind several obscene pictures. He said that he had never been able to forget them. Even at the Communion Table, they sometimes appeared before his eyes and filled him with shame.

It is a dreadful thing to hang evil pictures in a boy's mind. Many men have been guilty of it. One thinks of the barrack room and the old soldier pouring out his fund of foul reminiscence, and the young recruits lapping it up. One thinks of the workshop and men in middle life passing on some obscene titbit to the apprentice. They will share the guilt if those boys go wrong. It will be no answer to say that they did not lapse into immorality themselves. They excited and distorted a boy's imagination; they inflamed the lusts of youth; they made it harder for them to be decent, and they will share the shame if they sin.

Outside the dockyard gates at Portsmouth one day a friend of mine boldly challenged a man who was telling foul stories to a group of apprentices in the dinner hour. I was a witness of the incident myself. The man said, "Mind yer own business. They'll have to learn all about the world and it will make men of them." My friend looked him in the eye and said: "Very good! And if, when you have made men of them, one of them should seduce your daughter, I hope you will admire the kind of manhood that you've made." I can still see the look on the story-teller's face. My friend's sword had pierced his armor. The hooter went and, in conscious guilt, he walked slowly back to work.

The lusts of the world are not only manufactured by the openly sensual. They are fostered by all who tell the bawdy tale, by all who snigger over some dirty bit of garbage which is going the round. Too cowardly to set their face and show that they are not amused, too weak to cut the sordid story-teller short, they lend their aid to vice and become the accessories of sin. The immorality of the world would be far less if there were less traffic in immoral tales. One can barely assess the harm that they do. The resources of Christ are at the call of any who are bent on purity and who are swift to meet any corruption in the conversation with a clean and lifting word.

Or perhaps that was not your error. You are far too genteel for that! But are you a dealer in idle and hurtful gossip? Many people who would not dream of telling an impure tale are willing to pass on a tainted hint, a bit of gossip, a lying rumor, and besmirch somebody's good name.

Shakespeare makes Iago say:

"Who steals my purse steals trash; 'tis something, nothing;
 'Twas mine, 'tis his, and has been slave to thousands;
 But he that filches from me my good name
 Robs me of that which not enriches him
 And makes me poor indeed."

Many people are engaged in that unholy traffic:

filching other people's good name and, by some bit of idle slander, making the burden of life more difficult for their neighbor to bear.

Look at this easy, deadly thing. How strange it is that a breath, a word, could be so fatal in its consequences! Notice how it feeds on trivialities, neglects the laws of evidence, and leaps to false conclusions.

During the Great War, gossip said that Mrs. Asquith (as she then was) was a pro-German and a danger to the State. It was not true. She simply sympathized with those who went to Donnington Hall to visit German officers who were imprisoned there and whose mothers they chanced to know. That was all. Gossip did the rest, and did it with such evil thoroughness that her life, and the life of her great husband, were plagued for years. One day, when the war was well over, she confessed to Mr. Asquith that she half wished that she had dropped her friends of German name and "never gone to say 'Good-bye' to those poor Lichnowskys," to which he replied: "God forbid! I would rather ten thousand times be out of public life forever."

Gossip said in 1877 that Dr. Barnardo was a thief, a brute, a charlatan, and an immoral monster. Gossip even went to the unusual length of setting out the charges in a shilling booklet of sixty-two pages. It was said that he had been seen with a prostitute on his arm. It was true! He was leading the poor wanton to a rescue home. It was said that he called himself "Doctor" when he had no *legal* right to the term. It was true. But then, not one in ten of the medical men in England have a *legal* right to the term. They are bachelors of medicine and licentiates in surgery. Only a small percentage proceed to the M.D. Custom confers the general title and Barnardo had as clear a claim to it as the majority of his professional confreres. It was a foul slander to call him a "charlatan." The other charges were just as hollow. Gossip made them. A board was appointed to inquire into them, and Barnardo was proved to be the unstained champion of the outcast child.

John Stuart Mill, the philosopher, was a bachelor of retiring habits. During his scholarly researches he met a certain Mrs. Taylor, a lady of considerable mental power, and a friendship sprang up between them. It was a friendship in study, as antiseptic as an operating theater and including no element of evil at all. But gossip got busy with it. The tongues of the scandal-mongers wagged, and poor Mill, who was almost ceasing to be a recluse, drew back into his shell again. Ostracized by gossip. Life made unendurable by the fetid hint and the poisoned word.

One of the worst things about gossip is that it is so seldom possible to get to its source. It is like trying to put a cloud of smoke into a bottle. You cannot grasp anything; you clutch at it, but when you open your hand there is nothing there. Yet, all the time, it is in the atmosphere, choking the throat and making the eyes smart and swim. Once abroad, it is almost impossible to destroy, even by those who made it.

"Where there is so much smoke," people say, "there is sure to be at least a little flame."

After the war, a large quantity of the irritant Blue

Cross gas remained in a munition factory near Cologne. The city fathers, troubled by its dangerous possibilities, were concerned to destroy it, but the task has proved impossible. They tried to burn it, but it caused inconvenience to the country folk and affected vegetation. They buried it, but the fear arose that it would affect the subsoil water. It was proposed to sink it at sea, but the transport down the Rhine was judged to be too dangerous. In the passing of years it has been neutralized, burned, buried, disinterred, and reburied, and still it gives the custodians of the city no rest. At present it lies beneath the sods in an immense concrete "coffin" in the Whaner Moor, and the Moor has been closed and will remain so for thirty years. To make poison gas is not really difficult, but to destroy it defeats the ingenuity of experts.

It is not dissimilar with gossip. It is vaporous and so easily made, but it is deadly. One is never sure that one has it all, or has it firm. Somebody knows somebody who says that somebody saw . . . !

How can this evil thing be destroyed? By what discipline of heart and tongue can Jesus secure his servants from this common and malign sin?

Surely in ways like these. He deepens our love of *all* people. So many folks have told me that the surrender of their heart to Christ had this immediate consequence that I now expect to hear every new disciple say so. Many men and women have resentments against society, and feel that they are compassed about with those who plan their hurt. Even if their love of their own dear ones is deep, it is a narrow and particular love. The entry of Jesus into the heart vastly widens the scope of love. In place of suspicion and a bias to believe the worst of others, there come the most compassionate thoughts and a readiness to believe the best. Evil gossip cannot live with this love. A crowd is a moving sight to one full of affection for Christ. The heart swells with a desire to help, and all the nobler possibilities of human nature are in view.

Love is like that. Paul said, "Love is always eager to believe the best." When our neighbor's child is cross and peevish, we are tempted to complain about the nasty temper and ill training of the child. When our own child is cross and peevish, we say that he is unwell or overtired. That is the ingenuity of love. When Christ widens the love in us to include all for whom he died, gossip is killed. Our bias is to believe the best. Even when we cannot close our eyes to the evil of others, it is still possible to close our mouths.

And surely it was the love of Christ which moved the old saint of years ago to determine that he would never pass on any critical judgment of others until he had subjected it to a threefold challenge. He would ask himself: "Is it true? Is it necessary? Is it kind?"

Not many hurtful tales can pass that triple guard!

Is it true? "A friend has told you in confidence. . . . ?" "A near relation has let the news slip. . . . ?" "An intimate of hers got it on good authority. . . . ?" This will not do. Do you know *that* it is true?

If it is true, *is it necessary?* Will any good be done by the repetition? Is it essential that someone be

129

warned? Will more harm be done by silence than by speech?

Finally, *is it kind?* You are a sinner yourself. If God was swift to mark your many sins, what word could you say in denial or extenuation? Have you any hope at all, but in that mercy which finds expression in the Cross? You want God to be kind to you. Be kind to others. Seal your lips unless, by sealing them, you put another soul in jeopardy.

When sin contrives to cloak itself, Christ can still warn us of its presence and save us, not only from casting the stone, but from minding the coats.

XII

WHEN THE PROUD MAN FROM HIS PRIDE STOOPS . . .

It is always a matter of some surprise to ordinary people that theologians insist on the deadly nature of the sin of pride. The man in the street is disposed to say, "I know many sins more deadly than pride. There is greed, lying, lust; there is envy; there is murder; all these are more deadly sins than the sin of pride."

Nevertheless, there can be little doubt that the theologians are right. Pride is a deadly sin: indeed, there is some evidence for believing that it is the most deadly of all the deadly sins. The great St. Augustine held that view, and by common consent he was among the keenest thinkers in the world of his time. He believed that obstinate pride was the unpardonable sin itself. Thomas Aquinas, the most profound theologian of the middle ages, held that view also. "It is the deadliest of the deadly sins," he said. Dante shared the conviction too. However improbable it may seem to the lay mind that pride could be as heinous as these old thinkers believed, it cannot be denied that weighty opinion supports the view. Far, far greater than these is the judgment of Jesus himself. There is not much doubt that Jesus looked upon pride as among the deadliest of the deadly sins.

"But pride is such a harmless thing," men say. "A man who thinks a great deal about himself and keeps asking, 'Do you know who I am? Do you know what offices I have held?' . . . well, he may look silly, but he does not do any harm, not like a murderer, or a seducer, or a thief."

Indeed, there are some forms of pride, it is affirmed, which are positively good. "It is a good thing for a man to have pride in his family, in his country, in his friends, in his work. A man without any pride is a mean and inconsiderable creature, beneath the respect of normal men. It is only unworldly doctrinaires who would look upon pride as a vicious sin."

The heart of this grave sin is just here; that a man or woman thrust himself, or herself, right into the center of the picture and make themselves the test, and standard, and measure of all things. It is rather odd that it is necessary to state it, but man's place in the universe is that of a creature. The discerning and truthful mind says, "It is God that hath made us, and not we ourselves; we are his people, and the sheep of his pasture." But that is only the person of discernment. The pride of man rebels against his place in the universe. Protagoras cries, "Man is the measure of all things," and Henley bawls out in his blatant way:

> "I am the master of my fate,
> I am the captain of my soul."

Now that is the real germ of this soul disease. It puts self in the center. It struts, and shouts, and brags. It strikes an attitude. It says, "I . . . I . . . I . . ." It dethrones the Creator in the heart of man. It makes the puffed up little ego the pole of all things. It blackens this fair earth from end to end. If men only knew the thousand sins which pride begets, they would hate it for the devilish thing that it is.

Notice, first, that it is the enemy of love because "love vaunteth not itself, it is not puffed up." Love never thrusts itself to the center of the picture.

It builds barriers between the classes and makes Bolshevists of despised men. When one reads the biographies of the great revolutionaries, it is astonishing to notice how many of them have been directed to their vocation by some exhibition of class pride. Take the instance of Madame Roland, one of the leaders of the French Revolution, and a woman who enjoyed a great reputation as a friend of the people. Her memoirs make it perfectly clear that it was not simply a passion for the unprivileged which made her the revolutionary she was. One must go back in her life to the time when she had occasion to visit an aristocratic château, and the lordly owner of the place said, "Show her into the servants' hall." She never forgot his snub, and it made her a revolutionary. That is one chief way in which revolutionaries are made. They are products of the snobbish pride of other men.

Pride builds national barriers too. Inordinate pride of race in Germany is one of the reasons why hundreds of cultured Jews have been driven from her borders. It is crude national egotism, the worship of themselves. Some people find it hard to understand why there is so much anti-British feeling in India, but part of the explanation is to be found in the egotistic pride of those Englishmen who strut, and talk contemptuously of a man like Mr. Gandhi as a "half-naked nigger." The bill always comes in for such ebullitions of beastly pride. This voice is no harmless little idiosyncrasy. It is of the devil. The old theologians knew what they were about when they called it the deadliest of the deadly sins.

Let me indicate other ways in which this sin works out its evil course. I remember a quarrel I tried to heal a dozen years ago between two friends. As is so often the case, there were faults on both sides. In the heat of their anger hard things had been said, and the gulf was deep and wide when I sought to draw them together. Some of the trouble was cleared up very soon. Things that each had believed about the other were proved untrue and, as I ran between them, my hopes soared high that a reconciliation could be effected. But I failed at the last. Hours of patient labor came to nought. When we reached the point at which one or other of them should make an advance, and reach out the hand of fellowship, neither of them would do it. Like two silly girls they both said, "I will if he will, but I won't be first." It was pride; hateful, hurtful, hideous pride. They are estranged to this day, their old and lovely friendship blighted, because neither of them would sacrifice a bit of pride.

And if it is a pitiful thing that a man should miss the fellowship of his friend because of pride, how much more pitiful it is that a man or woman should miss the richness of God's fellowship for the same reason. It is one of the bitterest experiences of the minister that when he has made the way of life clear to a man, and set the love of Christ before him in as attractive a fash-

ion as is possible, he refuses him at the last because of
pride. That is always the last barrier to surrender, our
own stubborn pride which says, "We will not have this
Man to rule over us"; the craving to be the captain in
one's own life; the unwillingness to admit that we are
not our own, though we were bought with a price.
Many folks have missed God because of that. Oh the
peace we often forfeit and the needless pain we bear
. . . because of pride!

Nor does the evil entail of this sin end even there.
It is unique in the category of sins in that it is the only
sin which definitely derives occasion from our virtues.
It fixes its snare, not chiefly in the paths of vice, but
in the path of probity. It is distinguished in the number
of genuinely good people it enthralls. Lust requires a
foul mind in which to flourish. People who commonly
practice lying are all compounded of deceit. Most sins
spring up in the soil of sin, but pride has this peculiarity that it propagates itself in the soil of virtue too.
It seduces men and women who are nigh to being saints.
It can insinuate itself into the holy place, and catch
people out on their knees. How astonishingly easy it is
for a good man to believe that he is the author of his
own goodness. The man who has regulated his prayer
life, overcome greed by generosity, overcome passion by
self-discipline, and made his life a plain example of the
Ten Commandments, has one great snare left: he will
be tempted to believe that he has done it all himself.
Unless he keeps his eyes fixed upon the Cross, he will
begin to believe that he is the architect of his own
virtue. Self will strut back into the center again. Pride

will puff him up. He will stand in the temple of God as the Pharisee did, and pray thus "with himself": "God, I thank thee that I am not as other men are, extortioners, unjust, adulterers, or even as this publican. I fast twice in the week. I give tithes of all I possess."

And it was all true. He was not a liar. He was not an extortioner. Injustice could not be laid to his charge, nor yet adultery. He fasted twice in the week. (However hearty his appetite, he curbed it Monday and Thursday with a fast!) He gave tithes of all he possessed. (How many Christians give at least a tenth?) He subjected himself to as rigorous a code of rules as is known outside asceticism . . . and then spoiled it all by spiritual pride. Jesus said that the publican who beat his breast and moaned, "God be merciful to me a sinner," went down justified rather than the other. One had God still in the center. The other had . . . himself.

How can people think lightly of a sin which betrays them into superior, and sometimes contemptuous, feelings for others? Jesus never made light of the sins of the flesh, but he spoke to the spiritual pride of the Pharisees when he said, "The publicans and harlots go into the Kingdom of Heaven before you."

Nor does the danger of pride end even here. Not only does pride contaminate the virtues: it contaminates the other vices as well. Sin is ugly at any time, but is there anything more unspeakable than sin which takes pride in itself? Sin that is penitent, that falls to the ground and begs forgiveness, that sobs its way to the foot of the Cross—that sin is not a problem. Jesus dealt with that. In his name, the preacher can deal with it, all day, and every day. He will say to the weeping penitent, "Lift up your eyes. Look at your crucified Lord.

" 'Pardon for all flows from His side;
My Lord, my Love is crucified.' "

To point the penitent to pardon is payment enough for all the toil of ministerial service.

" 'Tis worth living for, this,
To administer bliss
And salvation in Jesus' name."

But what will you do with the man or woman who takes pride in his sin?

Think, for instance, of a mean man. Meanness is a nasty sin, yet one has nothing but sympathy for a man who is struggling against it. One's heart goes out to him if he says, "I am striving against my niggardliness. Money was scarce in my home when I was a child, and I grew up careful of every copper. Now that I have plenty, I cannot bear to part with it. I know I am mean. I hate myself for it, but I hope to overcome."

If a man speaks like that from his heart, one is full of sympathy for him. He has a right to words of encouragement, and the assurance that God will give him the spirit of generosity.

But what can we say of a man who takes pride in his meanness; who has a thirst when his pals are paying and an appointment when his own turn comes round; who tells the story afterwards with gusto, and leads the laugh against his simple friends? I heard of such a man recently. He had been for an expensive continental holiday and had just returned to London. A couple of days after his return, a blind man accosted him in the streets and asked him for a coin. He had a franc in his pocket, worthless now to him and to the beggar, but he put the franc in the blind man's palm. Telling the story afterwards, with many a chuckle, he said: "He felt the milled edge and thought it was a shilling. He thanked me profusely."

The bounder! The mean, contemptible skinflint! Is it not clear what he has done? He has added pride to his meanness and made it immeasurably worse. Pride is like that. It not only contaminates the virtues: it contaminates the other vices as well.

Nor can I forget the conceited harlot whom a friend of mine generously tried to help. Not that she felt any need of help. There was no penitence in her, or shame of her unmentionable life. She met my friend's gentle offer of assistance with the hauteur of a duchess, and said, "Of course, it is only the upper class that I serve." My God! The upper class! Oh, I know how to deal with the Mary Magdalenes, when all the foulness of their life breaks over them, and they cannot believe that there is a way back to purity and peace. I say, "Take my arm, sister. Take my arm. I am an unprofitable servant myself. Come! I know the way to the Cross."

But what can one do with a proud painted strumpet like that, who struts about with a supercilious air and would despise a factory girl who had kept her body as a temple of the Holy Ghost? There is nothing one can do. Pride possesses her sinful soul, and pride has this terrible quality that it blocks the way to Calvary.

Were the old theologians right then, when they called this the deadliest of the deadly sins? It is clear that they were more right than many were willing to concede. The core of it sounds so harmless when it is simply expressed as putting self in the center, and not God. But what iniquity flows from that transposition. Pride fights against love; it builds barriers between the social classes; it builds barriers between the nations; it prevents reconciliation; it blocks the way to Calvary; it poisons the virtues; it doubles the viciousness of the vices; in short, *it is hell to have self in the center and not God*. Who can deliver us from pride, the outer rind and the endless inner casings? An old saint once said: "Ridding ourself of pride is like peeling an onion; every skin one takes off, there is another skin beneath." Christ is able. Only Christ. He can rid the soul of pride. He kneels at the feet of Judas, girded with a towel, and washes the traitor's feet. No show acting. Just a simple service rendered to a man who had tramped about dusty roads all day in sandals. "God of God. Light of Light. Very God of Very God. Begotten, not made" . . . washing feet.

Yet, it may be that a doubt as to the deadly character of pride still remains. Is it *all* illegitimate? Is no pride pardonable? Cannot a man be proud of a fine family, or school, or nation, or friend? Cannot a mother be proud of her children, or a workman of his craft?

When people make this plea they are confusing two things, two things which look alike but are poles apart.

Let us illustrate from a young man's love of his old school. Here are two men, both of whom went to the same school, but how differently they speak of it. One of them thrusts it upon you. He wears the old school tie, and contrives to give you the impression that you went to the wrong school. He says, "I went to Bifton. It is a public school, you know. It was admitted to the Headmasters' Conference last year. That makes it a public school. We have nobody who is in trade at Bifton. I am an old Biftonian."

How nauseating tattle like that sounds to any normal man. The company of such a braggart is boring beyond words. Under one's breath, one says, "If that is Bifton, give me Borstal."

But here is the other young man. He went to the same school. He never says, "I am an old Biftonian." He does not think much of himself: he thinks of the school, her fine past, her great record of service, and her sons worthily bearing responsibility in all corners of the world. As he muses, an intense longing rises in his heart, strangely blended of privilege and responsibility, and half under his breath he says, "May I be worthy of my old school."

Now these two states of mind may have a superficial resemblance, but they are distinct and, indeed, opposed. The first man is an insufferable prig, whose oozing pride so soon disgusts you. The second unconsciously commands your respect, because he is clearly a gentleman. He does not obtrude himself. Beyond and above himself he sees a great tradition, and walks with quiet dignity as one who would be worthy of it.

It is a mistake to call the second state of mind "pride." It is definitely not pride. However much ordinary people may deny the theologian's dictum, they come into line with him at the last because they have a hearty dislike of pride and, when they admire, it is not pride that wins their admiration, but this other attitude of heart. It is clearly distinguished from pride because self is not at the center. The mind has been captured by a great purpose, and the whole personality is knit together in service. At the center is the cause, and on the circumference is the self. But self is satisfied. Little as the egotists realize it, we are so made that there is interior peace only for those who live for some great cause outside themselves.

How drastically Christ deals with pride, all Christian biography is witness. Humility is the mark of the saint in every branch of the Church. Only the ignorant confound it with the inferiority complex. They are not even related. The great saints have often been men and women of great gifts and great achievements, but Christ plucked out the pride in their soul and replaced it with humility.

John Wesley, as a youth, called on Dr. Sacheverell with a letter of introduction from his father. "I found him," said Wesley, "as tall as a maypole and as proud as an archbishop. I was a very little fellow. He said, 'You are too young to go to the university. You can know no Greek or Latin yet. You go back to school.' I looked at him as David looked at Goliath and despised him in my heart. I thought, if I do not know Greek and Latin better than you I ought to go back to school indeed."

"I despised him in my heart." There speaks the youthful Wesley. He did not brag, but he looked, despite his lack of inches, as if he thought that he did not need to. Pride was his sin. But time went by, and grace well refined his heart. We find him, years later, dining, whenever he was in London and as long as the Foundry was his headquarters, in the poorhouse with the widows, the blind, the orphans, and the servants, on the same food and at the same table. He said, "We rejoice herein, as a comfortable earnest of our eating bread together in our Father's kingdom."

To tell of all those who have been distinguished in humility would be to transcribe the calendar of the saints, the calendar as they keep it in the Church Triumphant. One thinks of St. Francis and St. Teresa; of George Herbert and John Keble; of Alexander Whyte and John White of Mashonaland. Keble's biographer said that he had "a humbling humility." His gentle presence seemed to prick the puffed-up pride in the vainest soul. Alexander Whyte became almost a standard in this grace. Dr. Denney, in one of his letters, speaks of Dr. Smellie as the humblest man he knew "except Dr. Whyte."

Years ago, Edinburgh was shocked by the disgrace and imprisonment of one of her prominent citizens. In his vestry next Sunday morning, Dr. Whyte heard the church bells ringing, and he turned to his assistant minister and said, "Do you hear those bells? He hears them in his prison cell this morning. Man, it might have been me." [1]

The Cure D'Ars actually signed *himself* the letter of accusation laid against him by the neighboring priests. Before the bitter thing was sent to the Bishop, either from bravado or perhaps by mistake, a copy was sent to the accused man. He read it carefully, agreed with all it said about his folly, excess of zeal, and ignorance of theology, added his own signature, and returned the document. "He united himself with his accusers to gain a disgrace which he agreed with them in thinking he deserved." [2]

Pride is a deadly sin. Christ can cure it. Only Christ.

[1] *Alexander Whyte,* Barbour, pp. 562 f.
[2] *The Secret of Curé D'Ars,* Henri Ghéon, p. 129.

XIII

WHEN EVIL THOUGHTS MOLEST

I ONCE went to speak in the town of Bexhill-on-Sea and well remember a lovely avenue of trees I saw there. I think they were limes, but they were so tall and leafy that they seemed to rival in my imagination the famous avenue of chestnuts in Bushey Park.

But walking down the avenue I noticed a strange thing. Two of the trees standing side by side were dead, and not only dead, but dismally and evilly offensive. There seemed something sinister and cursed in their condition. Frost could not account for it: their neighbors were all healthy. There was no indication of blight: no noxious fly, it seemed, had fastened on their leaves. Those trees had enjoyed the same rain and warmth as every other tree in the avenue, and yet they were dead. So I made inquiries and this is what I found. A gas main ran underneath them . . . and it leaked! Everything on the surface had been in their favor, the breezes and the sunshine and soft refreshing rain. But they were dead because they had been poisoned from beneath.

There are men and women like that. The circumstances of their lives seem all in their favor, or at least only sufficiently awkward to bring out the best in them. They may have home, friends, comforts, encouragements, special advantages, and extra helps. Yet their lives are mysteriously blighted, and the finer fruits of spiritual growth never appear. Quite often they are poisoned from beneath. Their sad condition may remain a mystery to other people; but God, to whom all hearts are open, all desires known, and from whom no secrets are hid . . . God knows. They have not only been molested by evil thoughts but subjugated by them. They are the victims of a diseased imagination.

Sex is an absorbing subject, especially to the unmarried. It is grounded in our nature, and few topics can so engross the whole mind, or make this mortal nature burn with more curiosity. None but the abnormal are ignorant of this appetite, and only prudes and fools apologize for it. One might as well apologize for hunger.

Some people look upon the whole subject of sex as unclean, or at least as spiritually impoverishing. Even the Apostle Paul appears to do so.[1] Christianity, in the second stage of its struggle for life, had to combat the idea that sex was essentially unholy.[2] Tolstoy opposed the view that marriage is a Christian institution and argued that the true and unadulterated teaching of Christ did not form "a basis for the institution of marriage." He called marriage "domestic prostitution."[3] Gandhi's views are not widely different. He maintains that marriage should be an entirely spiritual alliance, and that the harmony of souls should not be disturbed by sexual relationship. Married couples are

[1] I Corinthians 7: 1-9.
[2] *New Morality*, Newsom, p. 19.
[3] Cp. *Epilogue of Kreutzer Sonata.*

admitted to Ashram only on condition that they live henceforth as brother and sister.

Yet, with the profoundest respect for these distinguished thinkers, it is impossible to share their views. To condemn an instinct as deep and wide as this is to condemn the Creator who made us and to desire a swift extinction of the race. Even as an immediate consequence, it would mean the disappearance of the best stock and the constant increase of those who are less fitted to replenish the earth. Though it be true that there are physical facts about sex which no fine writing can alter, and no spiritualizations make other than they are, we believe that it was beautiful in God's intention and a sacramental consummation of love. Inspired by deep affection, and protected by the binding vows of marriage, it is both the fulfillment of nature and a pure gift of God.

Yet, it cannot be denied, however pure this relationship may be in essence and in the intention of God, it has been defiled in all kinds of ways, and has corrupted body, mind, and soul. The disproportion of the sexes denies this natural fulfillment to thousands of women; economic and other conditions impose long years of rigorous abnegation on thousands of men. People of a hot passionate nature, however high their ideals, have often to fight a long and difficult battle in their minds and imaginations. Evil thoughts molest. At least, if they are not evil in their inception, they are perilous in their development and often evil in their consequences. A certain thought comes to the mind, not unnaturally perhaps, having regard to our nature, but instead of being swiftly outmaneuvered and skillfully elbowed away, it is toyed with and gets further in. "I can dismiss it at any moment I like," thinks the poor fool, who nevertheless continues to finger it, and forgets that it is gathering volume with every minute that he gluts his imagination in it. So from inclination it passes to appetite, and from appetite to hunger, and from hunger to craving, and from craving to torment, and from torment to sin. The whole battle is fought in the mind. If it is lost, it is usually lost in the first few minutes. If it is lost repeatedly, the man becomes at last the kind of person of whom Montaigne speaks with much contempt, "a man whose head is a merry-go-round of lustful images."

Who can save us from this sin? Who knows our nature enough to sympathize and yet to triumph? Christ does! He is able! He was tempted in all points like as we are, yet without sin.

Nor is it hard to show the method of his success. This battle must be won in the mind. It is imperative that the imagination be healthy, and the thought stream filtered. Success here insures success all round.

So Christ aims to occupy the mind. His presence welcomed and enthroned affects every area of life and every tributary of thought; it guarantees that no chain of associated ideas shall lack a spiritual link; it purges, sweetens, enriches; it makes all things new.

Men's minds are affected by the literature they read. If they have a mind to it, it is not hard to lay hands on books filled with lustful images and calculated to inflame all the swelling passions of life. The present age

147

has seen a spate of such books outpoured, from the pornographic novel to the volumes of "daring disclosures," books which are heartily commended by the scavengers who delight in such delicacies because they are "really hot." Nor has there been of late any lack of books on sex written with a high and serious purpose, and aiming to inform and instruct any who were not already satiated with the subject. Not seldom they have been read by people other than those for whom they were intended, and by quickening curiosity and furnishing the imagination with further pictures, they have sometimes had results which were far from their author's mind.

Christ guides the reading of those whose mind he occupies. His residence in the heart serves as a director in all our traffic with books.

It has other consequences as well. It affects the company a man keeps, the pictures he sees, and the jokes he will listen to. Burns said himself that when he wished to compose a love-song, his recipe was to put himself on a "regimen of admiring a beautiful woman." He deliberately filled his mind with pictures which were dangerous to his passionate nature. His biographer remarks that "when it came to be often repeated, as it was, it cannot have tended to his peace of heart, or to the purity of his life." [4]

Centuries before, Augustine had essayed the same perilous path. He came to Carthage, with all its tinseled vice, and of set purpose began to coax his own carnal appetites. He says:

[4] *Burns*, Shairp, p. 161.

"I love not as yet, yet I love to love; and, with a hidden want, I abhorred myself that I wanted not. I searched about for something to love, in love with loving, and hating security, and a way not beset with snares."

He succeeded.

"I befouled, therefore, the spring of friendship with the filth of concupiscence and I dimmed its luster with the hell of lustfulness: and yet, foul and dishonorable as I was, I craved, through an excess of vanity, to be thought elegant and urbane. I fell precipitately then. . . ." [5]

All human experience goes to show the folly of playing with these deep desires. In certan natures they are not easily kept in check even by a strong will and divine help, and without either, together with a wanton quest of diversion in such paths, the way to sin is alarmingly short.

Christ in heart and mind is the safeguard. To him supremely the prayer may be offered,

> "Breathe through the heats of our desire
> Thy coolness and Thy balm."

Nor is it hard to understand the simple psychology of it. If a man builds within himself a strong picture of Jesus; if a regular part of his leisure is consecrated to such reading, meditation, and prayer as will make Christ clearer to his mind and dearer to his heart; if he develops a keen ear for the personal words of his Master and directs his life accordingly; if Christ becomes to him a living personality whose encouragements he

[5] *Confession Book* 3, Chap. I.

covets and whose disapproval he dreads, it is not hard to see what help that man will have in any moment of swift temptation. The minute the thought comes to his mind and is recognized, he looks to his Lord. Evil thoughts are not driven out by dwelling on them, even guiltily or prayerfully. It is bad tactics to direct sustained attention to them even in penitence, or as one plans improvement. The longer they are in the focus of attention, the deeper they are burned on the memory, and the more mental associations they make. They must be outwitted by swiftly directing the mind to some other absorbing theme. They cannot be dismissed with a peremptory word, but they can be elbowed out by some antagonistic and antiseptic idea. Hence the wisdom of knowing Jesus as a personal Friend, and turning the mind at once toward him. He is the center of all things pure. To think of him is to summon his aid. The heat of unbridled passion abates in the steady gaze of his searching eyes. The sin that seemed so seductive a moment before looks loathsome with Jesus consciously present. Coolness in place of heat, and serenity instead of gathering desire, are the reward of anyone as swift to turn to Christ as they are swift to recognize the carnal character of tainted thought.

Here, then, is a blessed by-product of every hour of Bible study, Church fellowship and prayer, meditation and browsing in the byways of Christian biography. It makes Jesus more real. It increases the strength of his appeal when, in the flashpoint of temptation, desire and opportunity having come both together, the trembling soul looks at once to its Lord and finds that he is able to save. Thousands of tempted men and women testify to his ability. Those who have been beaten before witness that "he breaks the power of canceled sin." He is able to beget in us that abnegation which God requires outside the marriage bond, and the continence he demands within it.

A further thought may be added here. It is not the least part of the service our Lord renders to us, that he reveals us to ourselves. We never really know the men and women we are until we see ourselves in him. During the war a soldier picked up on the battlefields of France a battered frame which had once contained a picture of Jesus. The picture had gone but the frame still bore the words *Ecce Homo*. The soldier sent it home as a souvenir, and someone at home put a mirror in it, and hung it on the wall. One day a man went into that house and read the startling words, *Behold the Man*, and saw *himself*. It is a parable. We see ourselves only when we see ourselves in Jesus. Blots we barely knew were there, come to view in his white light: the bias of our nature, the chinks in our armor, our temperamental weakness, he knows them all and shows us as we are able to bear. But what unique preparation for a battle with sin! To be warned beforehand what it is not wise for one to do, and of the situation which our peculiar disposition makes specially perilous. Only Christ can render such individual service to the heart, and constrain the whole life of his disciple in such ways as will not make the conflict with evil impossibly hard.

Nor does he fail, also, to offer his followers numberless simple aids to a pure life. Many men have found it helpful, in their efforts to outwit sin, not only to fix their mind on Jesus, but to use also, as lesser helps, any wholesome topic in which they have a specially keen interest. A University undergraduate told me once that, realizing that this battle had to be won in the mind, he was quick to escape a train of evil thoughts by thinking first of Christ, but also, by anticipation, of the graduation ceremony when he hoped to take his degree, and of certain fascinating things concerning his hobbies. Being deeply interested in each of these alternate themes, he had proved by experience that if he did not dally with the gross pictures which his imagination sometimes threw up, or which were thrust on him from outside, he could divert his mind by this means into interesting and clean channels. He was not singular in his experience. The mind bent on purity can find many a ruse to outmaneuver evil, but the surpreme Helper is Christ.

> "When evil thoughts molest,
> With this I shield my breast—
> May Jesus Christ be praised!"

With such strategy the wise disciple faces life. When Paul rehearses the things which are true, honorable, just, pure, lovely, and of good report, and then exhorts his readers to *think* on these things, the tempted follower of Jesus does not look upon the word "think" as an anticlimax. It is the acme of wisdom. To keep on thinking of these things is the only adequate preparation for the inevitable fight, and to think constantly of Jesus is to be the center of them all.

Nevertheless, freedom from defeat, here as elsewhere, is only possible by an unwearying vigilance. **Even ordered** thinking cannot entirely change our nature. The man who looks back over many victories and begins to assume that he is of finer clay than his neighbors, and essentially superior to the temptations which assail them, may receive, in his carelessness, emphatic proof that he is of the earth earthy.

The River Arun in Sussex used to enter the sea through a delta. In the passing of the centuries, however, all but one mouth of the river were closed up, and the river compelled, by artificial chalk banks, to reach the sea where men desired. What men could not alter, however, was the lay of the land, and always the river seemed to carry in its motion an ache for those forbidden channels where once it flowed.

Some years ago there was a heavy fall of snow in West Sussex, and a sudden thaw. Torrential rains and a driving wind coincided with the thaw, and one wild night the swollen river burst its man-made banks and sought again the license of its former days. A considerable part of the town of Littlehampton was flooded.

There is a similar turbulence beneath the curbed stream of many a consecrated life. There is no complete exemption from temptation. A sudden juxtaposition of events and the careless are caught napping. However rigid the mental discipline, it would be unwise in passionate natures to assume (if I may change the metaphor) that the volcanoes are quite extinct. That is what the people of Chile and Argentina mistakenly thought about the volcano of Descabezado. "It is extinct," they said. "No one living has seen a spark." And then, in April, 1932, it burst forth and with its awful pall of smoke blotted the sun from the heavens for towns that were fifty miles away, and shed a covering of ashes nearly three feet deep.

Only when one has hold of the hand of Christ is it possible to be anxious about nothing, and even that is not analogous to being careless about things. This is, in a special sense, a battle of the mind, and the apposite apostolic word is this: "Have this mind in you, which was also in Christ Jesus." To attain this mind may not be easy, but to be clear in one's aim, and constant in effort, should insure success.

XIV

WHEN I SEEK BUT FIND HIM NOT

ALL men to whom is intrusted the care of souls are familiar with the person who wants to find God, or be found by him, and cannot. The usual suggestions do not meet their needs, but their sincerity cannot be doubted. They are not of those who imagine themselves "mysterious" souls, and love to sit for hours and vaporize about their obscure thoughts. They are genuine seekers, and yet find some obdurate impediment to interior peace.

It is easily possible to turn them aside with some light word about the dangers of introspection, and assure them that if they say their prayers and do their duty, they will be all right. But such scant treatment does not reach the heart of their needs, and only adds perplexity to this keen hunger in their soul. One is often able to give them temporary encouragement by the reminder that God is the hunger, as well as the food, and convince them that deep longings after a higher life do not belong to raw human nature as such, but prove by themselves alone that God is already in their heart. The gloom they walk in is but the "shade of his hand outstretched caressingly." He, himself, put the keen edge upon their spiritual appetite. Did not Pascal say, "I had not sought thee hadst thou not already found me?"

Yet this encouragement is often only *temporary*.

They rightly think that God is able and ready to deliver them from a restless heart. They argue, cogently enough, that theirs is not a simple question of growth in grace, but something deeper and more original. They declare that they are not seeking a particular *kind* of experience, or profanely *demanding* of God the effervescent thrills and feelings which delight the immature. But they ask wistfully, earnestly, and honestly if it is not a fact that those who are found of God have quiet deep joys, a sense of power, and (most of all) an inner peace.

To all such questions there is only one answer. They have! That is not to say that those who have found God, and been found of him, never sink below the best, or slip into sin. They do. But they do not wallow. They get up facing the Cross—and go on. At times they must needs parry the assaults of doubt and fear, and sometimes the power of canceled sin proves not completely broken in their soul, but it is still true that joy, and power, and peace, are their portion. At the core of their heart they are content or, at least, their discontent is never elemental. It concerns themselves and never their Lord. They are satisfied with Jesus. Having met him, and given him their heart, they know that they can never really go back again. Matthew Arnold believed that there existed a peace of God "man did not make and cannot mar." These people do not merely believe it. They enjoy it. The seekers say, "Did God mean that peace for me?" We answer confidently, "He meant it for you."

But how can they find it? If God is seeking them

156

and they are seeking God, what hinders the meeting? Clearly, it must be something unsuspected in themselves. If they are not deliberately indulging in any known sin, or consciously resting God at some point where he has a plain controversy with them, the barrier must be hidden. Is Jesus able to reveal it? Can he turn a searchlight on all the complexities of the inner life and reveal the obstruction?

He is able!

It is a high privilege to work with Christ in the service of the seekers. One must often be prodigal with time, but the reward is rich. Thinking, talking, praying, and quietly listening to Jesus, the barrier finally appears. It often surprises the people themselves to discover what the impediment has been, and its removal may not be easy, but more than half the work is done when one knows what it is. Let me tell of some of the barriers which I have found, and illustrate them with experiences which the people who had them have kindly allowed me to use.

I have found in many minds a latent *condition* in all their dealings with God. Beneath all their praying— and a seeker is often most earnest in prayer—there is an unexpressed condition. All the promises they make to God—and some of their promises are most fervent— are really hypotheticals. "If this . . . then that." It is surprising that such a condition could be half-unconscious, and yet it often is.

Here is a young man who has been ill for four years —very ill. Before his sickness, he loved all sports and played several outdoor games keenly and well. Then he was laid on his back, and has been on his back most of the time since. Hope and despair of recovery have alternated in his mind. Brief periods of sitting out in the garden; longer periods on his back in bed. He had prayed to God, and God, he felt, had ignored him. Faith had all but gone and cynicism was taking its place.

In the quietness, one memorable day, after much thought and prayer, God showed us why his normal praying was unreal. A big condition lay beneath all his promises to God; a natural one, certainly, but God does not brook conditions. The only purpose of his praying, even when he did not mention it, was for health. Unexpressed, he was saying all the time, "If you make me better, Lord . . ." "If I can have my health again . . ." "If I can be as fit as my brother . . ." Tenderly, I told him where the flaw was, and nobly did he respond. Very moving was his prayer of dedication: "Lord, I have always come to you with 'ifs'; now I come to you with no 'ifs' at all."

He does not *suffer* his sickness now; he uses it. And God has gloriously used him.

Another instance of the same difficulty may be given here—a woman, full of Christian work, and effective up to a point, but who tried to hide a restless heart beneath a busy life. Few people could have suspected her need. I did not discover it myself until I had her resignation in my hands. The masquerade, she felt, had gone on long enough. Talking about God to others, when she was not intimate with him herself, was a form of hypocrisy she could not condone. She had had a wonderful experience of God years before; but now . . . Two or three weeks went by before we began to suspect the real trouble. Half-unconsciously she was making conditions with God. Friendship was her demand. Life was lonely for her. She lived alone and people left her alone. She seemed to know everyone, but coveted a special friend who could understand and sympathize. When she prayed, she pointed out to God her multitudinous services for him, and hinted to the Almighty that this merited some reward. But, as the sense of injustice grew in her heart, God seemed to recede, till she found herself busy in his service but really playing a part.

She did not hesitate when the true nature of her position was made clear to her. She knelt at the Cross, resurrendered her life, and borrowed the words of the saint—"It is not thy gifts that I desire. It is thyself."

Some are hindered by *fear*—fear in many forms. One man I remember was crippled by fear of infectious diseases, and another by a terrible fear of death. His description of his state of mind, when he had to undergo an operation, and face the fear that he might not come around, was almost terrifying. And the operation was quite a minor one.

Yet, as we looked into it quietly with God, it became clear that he had no real dread of physical death. He was not what the world would call a coward. He was afraid of God and of judgment. So the conversation led on to sin, and that was the heart of the matter. Sin! Not a growing pain, but a malignant growth. I offered the forgiveness of God and he took it—snatched it. How sweet he found it. I have never seen as much in the fifty-first Psalm as he saw. Now he lives to pass it on, and only marvels that men do not leap more swiftly to the release which he has found. In his own way, he says with Paul:

> "Oh could I tell ye surely would believe it!
> Oh could I only say what I have seen!
> How should I tell or how can ye receive it,
> How, till He bringeth you where I have been?"

While we are dealing with fear, another instance can be given here. It is singular, in my experience, though clearly it comes in this category. He was a young man, with real charm, and a keen seeker. The rich sense of God, which he noticed and admired in others, seemed always to pass him by. I suspected some sense of inferiority, and thought that his sarcasm was a mere defense, but this did not bring us to the heart of the problem. Deeply embedded in his nature was a fear that God wanted him to be a minister. No call from God had come to him to seek ordination, but the idea had been sown in his mind since childhood, and it had become a bogey. He loathed the thought. He was never amused by a caricature of a curate. He saw himself in the pillory. It was fixed in his mind that if he surrendered to God, God would put a clerical collar round his neck.

Nor could one promise that God would do no such thing, however confident one felt upon the point oneself. He had to be willing even for that. Very hard, he found it, to say, "Put me to what thou wilt," but, when it was said, and all his life laid upon the altar, how quick the peace flooded in. Now he can laugh at his fears. God knows he is willing to do his bidding, but it is not to the ministry that he has been called. His hands are full of service as a layman; his inferiority has gone; he is no longer sarcastic. There is something singing inside him.

Another common barrier is *resentment*. It would seem at first that anybody who had a resentment in his heart would realize that that would be a barrier to God's indwelling, but experience shows that it is not quickly recognized as such, especially when the resentment has a just cause.

In the days when I was more immature in this work than I am now, I spent many valuable hours to help a man to a vivid awareness of God, and never mentioned the possibility of resentment to him. That I did so finally, I owe (as I believe) to the guidance of God. As I waited on God in the quietness, a sense of the character of this man's need came to me, and the moment I touched the spot, he winced. It was a great abscess full of impure matter, and the "Celestial Sergeon" had to lance it and press out the pus.

He brought me a bundle of anonymous letters and asked me to read them—foul things, full of libel on himself and on a dear one. Nor was he ignorant of their author. The chain of evidence was all but complete; he had taken advice from a solicitor, and he was just waiting . . . waiting . . . for revenge. He seemed to gloat on the letters, and said that they were worth more to him than the £200 which he had saved.

So we went to work. I showed him that, however

just the resentment might be, it was a poison at the heart of his life, and no peace could come till the passion for revenge had gone. He saw it all when we looked at the Cross. If resentment was ever justified, it would have been justified in Jesus. But he did not look down from the Cross upon the howling mob who had not the common decency to let him die in quietness, and say, "Are these the brutes for whom I am dying?" He said rather, "Father, forgive them; they know not what they do."

So he went home, burned the letters before he went to bed, and has been busy since trying to win the one who slandered him. It was a wonderful night when I saw them sitting together in church.

Pride is another common barrier. This deadly sin takes many forms and is skillful at disguises, but the peculiar form it took in a minister's wife is in my mind as I write. She had long sought the peace of God in vain, and was vaguely aware that the barrier was in herself, and yet she was transparently sincere in her assurance that she did not know what it was.

When pride was mentioned, she was emphatic that it was not that. Nor did it seem likely. She wore her gifts with disarming modesty, and kept a constant course equidistant between inferiority and conceit, and while it was probable that pride had its place in her somewhere, it did not seem possible that pride was the chief impediment to her peace.

Yet it proved to be pride in the end; not pride in herself, but pride in her husband. It is among the peculiarities of this vice that it can wear a white robe and masquerade as love, or loyalty, or patriotism, or parental care. It was compounded of love and loyalty in her case. She wanted the Kingdom of Heaven to come, but she wanted her husband to have a prominent share in its coming. It made her avid for his praise, and swiftly and heatedly defensive if the value of his work was impugned. Meanwhile, the background of her thought was this, that he was *her* husband.

Christ made it clear to her in the quietness, and she did not falter long when she saw how sin had trapped her. To be true, she did attempt some weak defense of her state of mind, and pleaded that there is a "proper pride," but it was not hard to convince her that she was confusing two similar but disparate things. She does not love her husband less, now that she loves Christ and the Kingdom more. Her honest and eager praise of other people's success is good to hear, and the peace of God garrisons her heart.

Finally, it may not be unprofitable to mention again how often theoretical difficulties of the Christian faith are made half-consciously into a screen to hide some moral failure. That there are many acute intellectual problems in religion cannot be denied, and it would be an arrogant impertinence even to hint that all people who are hindered by these problems are consciously or unconsciously using them as a screen.

Nevertheless, it is the experience of all men and women who aim to aid their fellows to a rich experience of God, that many people who sincerely believe that the Virgin Birth, or the physical Resurrection, or the problem of suffering is the barrier to faith, are really impeded by some personal defeat in their own interior life, and are using the intellectual difficulties as a "defense mechanism." The rationalizations we employ vary with our mental furniture, but people of an inter-B.Sc. mind usually make them out of intellectual perplexities. It would he humble, and might be eternally profitable, if those people who feel that the barrier to faith is the unscientific character of religion would look closely at the whole matter again, preferably in the company of a confidential and wise Christian friend.

Other barriers are as common as those I have mentioned, and some are quite peculiar to the person concerned. Some stories can never be told, not even with permission, but Christ is able and willing to reveal the obstacle to any honest heart. He will not withstand the plea of the hymn writer:

> "Jesus, the hindrance show,
>   Which I have feared to see,
> Yet let me now consent to know
>   What keeps me out of Thee."

In the instances I have given, I have omitted the complicating details and made them appear more simple than they were. Nor have I attempted to give, in these few examples, a complete list of all those submerged obstructions, for they are legion. But these instances will fulfill their purpose if they show, first, that sincere people are often ignorant of the real problem of their own life, and, secondly, that Christ is both able to find it, and take it away.

XV

WHEN I FIND IT HARD TO PRAY

ONE day a university student came to see me on the matter of prayer. He reminded me of an address which I had given recently and asked whether he had understood me aright that John Henry Newman and Andrew Bonar both gave two hours a day to prayer. I said he had heard me correctly. I went on to say that there was nothing singular about that so far as the saints were concerned, and talked to him of the devotional habits of other people who hungered and thirsted after righteousness and how, despite their exceedingly busy lives, they were prodigal with hours spent in prayer.

His bewilderment grew. "What beats me," he said, "is how they filled up the times. It is hard to imagine how men with many duties to do could give the *amount* of time to it, but it is still harder to know they used it, once it was set aside. I can't pray for ten minutes. I've tried. I kneel down every night and just ask God to forgive me for anything I've done wrong. I thank him for his blessings. I mention mother and father and my other relations. I say a word about my friends, and the Church, and then I'm done. Sometimes I stay a bit longer, but my mind keeps going off at a tangent and I've nothing more to say. Five minutes covers it. How people can pray for two hours beats me."

The perplexity of that young man is a very common one. It is not to be confused with doubts about the theory and efficacy of prayer: it is a matter of method and practice. Many folks who have no difficulty about the duty and value of devotion and who are not barring their own way by deliberate indulgence in known sin fail in the *act* of prayer. Some who have been Christians for years are still in the kindergarten of this school and, seeing that prayer is the very heart of the devotional life, their spiritual progress clearly depends on learning how to pray. In the days of his flesh, his disciples said, "Lord, teach us to pray."

He is able to teach us still.

The obstacles to prayer are many, though some are mere excuses and would quickly yield to a resolute act of will. There is the difficulty about *time*. People complain that their busy lives give them no time for prayer, but it is usually a shallow evasion because they clearly find time for less important things—the newspaper and amusements. No one deeply in love would fail to find time for a daily word with the loved one, if the loved one lived at hand. Christ stole time from his sleep to pray. Wesley rose every day at 4 A.M. for the same purpose. Francis Asbury was astir at five. The first thing in the morning is the best time for prayer, but if peculiar circumstances really make that impossible, the keen mind will find time before the day is old. One of the busiest women I have ever known, a working-class woman with a large family, keeps her tryst with God in the early afternoon when the last member of the family has returned from the midday meal. Before beginning again, she reads the book of God and spends time in unhurried prayer. "Then," she says, "I wire in again." It is not always possible for a will to find a way, but it *is* possible in the matter of prayer. Time *can* be found. One could begin with a minimum rule of fifteen minutes each day. Even so slight an investment of well-used time would bring a vast and precious gain.

Then there is the difficulty about *place*. If it is possible, it is glorious to have a little oratory in the home, some private spot kept for devotions and marked by a sacred picture or symbol. Such a spot gathers associations, and calls us to prayer even when inclination ebbs.

But that is not always possible. In overcrowded homes privacy is hard to find, and people complain that this prevents them from praying. It need not. Let them start earlier for work and slip into a church and pray there. And let them strive to build an oratory within their heart, a sacred silence inside them, to which they can retreat in the midst of noise and chatter. It is astonishing how real a secret chamber can be built within the heart by imagination and consecrated thought. In an overcrowded room, in a bus, or train, or tram, the mind can learn by practice how to be deaf to all distractions and climb the hidden stair to the sacred place; a chapel, a quiet room, a garden, howsoever one has pictured it, but where Jesus abides and greets you with a smile, and says, "You have come." The saints have long known the secret.

When Charles de Foucauld was living his hermit life

in the deserts of North Africa, he was sometimes invited by the French officers to their mess. He went. At table he was the center of all whosesome fun. Story followed story, and Foucauld laughed with the rest. But as the evening wore on, the company would get more than merry. Perhaps the Colonel's stories passed the limit of propriety, and then Foucauld, judging a public rebuke ill-timed, left the fellowship. He still sat at the table, but he withdrew himself to the secret chamber of his soul. He dropped out. He did not hear. He thought of other things. Quite often, someone would notice and remark that the father must be scandalized, but the hermit-saint waved their excuses aside. "I was not listening," he would say. "I did not hear." And it was true. He was in his oratory, the oratory which any man can build within his soul.

Nor should it be forgotten, by those whose prayers are hindered by the lack of privacy, that it is always possible to go for a walk with Jesus. What conversation one can have with Christ on a lonely walk! Who does not know of the walk that Alexander Whyte had with God during his Christmas holiday at Bonskeid, "the best strength, and the best sweetness of all my Christmas holiday"? And how, after eight cold miles, he saw at last Schiehallion clothed in white from top to bottom, and poured out his soul as David did: "Wash me, and I shall be whiter than snow." Who does not remember how he walked back under the rising moon with his heart in a flame of prayer?

"Where'er we seek Thee Thou art found,
And every place is hallowed ground."

Some people complain that they are too *weary* to pray. Inquiry shows that this excuse is made by those who leave their prayers to the end of a tired day. It is both irreverent, and unprofitable, to treat our devotions in such a fashion. The majority of us come to our beds heavy with fatigue, and some final act of committal is the most we are capable of. "Into thy hands, O Lord, I commend my spirit." If our serious prayer is all left till then, it is small wonder if we find it a burden, and fall asleep as we pray.

"Rabbi" Duncan, at one time professor of Hebrew in New College, Edinburgh, and a man of vast learning in the Oriental tongues, was suspected by his students of offering his private prayers in Hebrew. It is said that two of them determined to prove the truth or falsity of this rumor by listening outside his bedroom door just after he had retired for the night. Everything went according to plan. They heard the old scholar potter about his room for some minutes, and then kneel to pray. But it was no Hebrew that came. The erudite old saint just said:

> "Gentle Jesus, meek and mild,
> Look upon a little child,
> Pity my simplicity,
> Suffer me to come to Thee. Amen!"

That was all. His deep prayer had been offered earlier in the day, and with a fresh mind. He committed himself to God at the last with the simple words of childhood. The listeners heard the bed creak and knew that "Rabbi" Duncan had gone to sleep. Reverence,

as well as the simple sense of the thing, demands that
we pray before we are too weary to pray well.

Lack of imagination and an undisciplined mind are
also obstacles to prayer. Building a chapel in the soul,
for which we have pleaded, seems impossible to people deficient in imagination and, if imagination built
it, their inability to concentrate would make it difficult for them to worship there. The great Bishop Butler
certainly assumed "a license in the use of words" when
he derided imagination. It is a great gift of God to
men. Modern psychology is emphatic on the point.
To see the unseen by an effort of the mind; to look at
Jesus; to be present (as Ruskin said) "as if in the
body, at every recorded event in the history of the
Redeemer." This gives a wing to earth-born creatures
and scales the heights of heaven. What need there is to
exercise imagination in prayer! The man who feels that
he is merely speaking into space soon ceases to speak at all.
The man who both reads his Bible and prays with imagination finds the book become autobiographic and
his prayers a deep delight. It is a sanctified imagination which would revolutionize the devotions of many
people. If they lived *in* the Gospels and felt themselves
the leper whom Jesus healed, the blind man whose sight
he restored, the dying thief whom he pardoned, the
disciples who first heard that he had risen from the dead,
what a delight the book would become! And if they
turned in that spirit to prayer, and *saw* him, how swiftly the prayer would flow. The Psalmist said, "I have
set the Lord always before me." So can the simplest
soul. Imagination was given to us that while yet on

earth, we might mingle with the heavenly throng. We close our eyes in prayer that we might open them to glory. Let us *see* God, and prayer will break from us as the water gushed from the rock.

Lady Tennyson had a lovely face. Even the scornful housemaid who contemptuously referred to her master, the poet, as "only a public writer," said of her mistress, "Oh she is an angel." Tennyson himself remarked one night to a friend, after his wife had gone to bed, "It is a tender, spiritual face." Her looks matched her spirit, and her sanctity was outstanding even in an age of formal goodness. She knew the use of imagination in prayer. She told her husband once: "When I pray, I see the face of God smiling upon me."

Let no beginner in prayer abandon the privilege because of mind wandering. It can be conquered. A quickened imagination and a resolute will cannot be denied. Even though, in the early stages, the precious minutes tick away and all the time seems spent in bringing the mind back from its wanderings and fixing it again on prayer, they are not moments lost. Such discipline will exercise the muscles of the will, and the day will dawn when the sweetest meditation and the most earnest prayer will be possible even amid distraction.

Enslavement to feeling is another fruitful cause of neglected prayer. People do not pray because they do not feel like it, and they offer the excuse with a certain cheerful assurance that it will be accepted. They assume that prayers are only efficacious when they rise from an eager and emotional heart.

Nothing could be further from the truth. Many of

the saints believe that floods of feeling belong only to the elementary stages of discipleship. All of them agree that we must keep our appointments with God, whether we feel like it or not. The most noble and enjoyable vocations bring their times of drudgery. If life were lived on a basis of feeling alone, nothing would be stable; appointments would not be kept; morality would be undermined; caprice would dethrone order in this world. If we have an engagement with a friend at a certain hour, we keep it, however disinclined we may feel when the time comes. Are we to be less courteous with God?

Nor should it be forgotten that God can do more for us, when we pray against inclination, than when we pray with it. The meek submission of our will deepens our surrender: our resolution to engage in prayer strengthens thought control. We rise from such prayers infinitely stronger than if we had knelt only at the dictate of desire. Faith, not feeling, measures the efficacy of prayer. Jesus never said, "Thy feeling hath made thee whole." He put the emphasis always on faith, and faith receives a finer witness when we pray against inclination than when we pray with it.

Too much stress upon speaking is the final common obstacle that we will mention. People unpracticed in prayer suppose that no prayer is being offered unless they are talking all the time. They seem to know nothing of dumb adoration, or the silent rapture of gazing on those glorious scars. Augustine said that our prayers ought to contain not *multa locutio* but *multa precatio*—"not much speaking, but much prayer." The method of prayer taught by Studdert Kennedy was largely wordless. It depended on lifting pictures, by a devout imagination, from the gospels and gazing and gazing on them. None who has practiced it will deny its power. To join the company in the upper room and have one's feet washed by Jesus is an awesome experience, blasting the pride in our soul as by a great explosive.

There are times when speech is easy, and when one can pour out the heart to God in a torrent of words, with all the natural simplicity of a child talking to his father, but never let it be thought that prayer is only for the fluent. God forbid! The most inarticulate can pray. When grief, or disappointment, or sin strikes one dumb, devotion does not end. There is still the upward look. Even when one weeps, it is one thing to weep to oneself and another to weep to Christ.

All the world knows now of old Pére Chaffangeon, who used to remain for hours before the altar in the church at Ars, without even moving his lips; it seems that he was speaking to God.

"And what do you say to him?" the curé asked.

"Oh," replied the old peasant, "he looks at me, and I look at him."

"The greatest of mystics," says Henri Ghéon, "have found no formula more simple, more exact, more complete, more sublime, to express the conversation of the soul with God."

But let us turn from the obstacles, and our simple counsel on how they may be overcome, to the help which Christ offers, and by which the impulse to pray is nourished, and the duty lost in the delight. A few minutes spent with the Bible is usually a swift preparation for prayer. A short, unhurried meditation on some fragment of scripture, and then silence, quickens the spirit of devotion. George Müller of Bristol always approached his mighty prayers in that way, and claimed that it delivered him from mind-wandering.

Then think of the many aspects of prayer. The people who find their times of communion tedious often regard prayer as nothing more than asking for things. The many-sided nature of the devotional life is strange to them. There is adoration, the awesome, humbling obeisance of the self before God, the rapt gazing on glory when the soul soars "and time and sense seem all no more." There is confession. Not some trite phrase which bundles all our beastliness together, and skates lightly away saying, "Forgive me for anything I have done wrong," but a mind which pursues holiness with method, digs out the evil things inside us and, in the pure presence of God, looks and loathes. There is intercession. How any man with faith in prayer, and a heart to pity, can fail to fill an odd half-hour at any time in earnest intercession, is hard to understand. The burdens of mankind are so numerous and heavy, that those who do not intercede lack either faith in prayer or feeling for their fellows.

There is thanksgiving too. Addison declared that eternity was too short to utter all the gratitude of his heart, but most people leave it out entirely or dismiss it with a word. Hard to pray for ten minutes? In ten minutes one could hardly think of the things which demand thanksgiving, much less compass all the other aspects of prayer!

And if we leave petitions aside—and petitions can always look after themselves—there is still consecration, the fresh surrender of the heart to God. "That vow renewed shall daily hear." What joy to gather every wandering thought and put one's whole life on the altar. What inward rest to feel the wonder of acceptance anew.

And all these are only *some* of the aspects of prayer. A wider survey of the country to be covered would surely serve the folk who find a sparsity of thought when they pray.

Not only is prayer quickened as we dwell on its many-sidedness but, still more, as we dwell upon its efficacy. Think of what it does. It changes the most intractable stuff in the universe—human nature—and makes sinners into saints. It brings heaven to earth. It fights vice and fosters virtue. It succors souls in peril and becomes a password at the gate of death.

Prayer puts the sick, and the infirm, in the fore-front of those who fight the battle of God. No one has ceased to serve who thinks to pray. It will damp the delights of Heaven for some of us, when we dis-cover how much prayer did on earth, and remember that we prayed so little. A wounded soldier told me during the war that his convalescence at home had had one great pain for him. He witnessed his mother's anxiety for his brothers who were still at the front. He heard her prayers and saw her feverish anxiety con-cerning the postman. He saw the furrows deepen in her face when neither letter nor field card was put in her hand. "It made me think," he said, "how often I might have written myself when I was out there, but thoughtlessly put it off." The memory of his selfishness was a shadow on the joys of home.

The memory of our prayerlessness may be a shadow on the joys of heaven. It may be that the greatest thing which we can do for anybody is to pray for them.

If a man treasures up the singular answers to prayer which he has heard; if he practices prayer and has his own answers to treasure up with them, he will not lapse into doubt. The experiment will end in an experience. There are many, many theoretical difficulties about prayer, but they are only academic questions to the people who pray. They *know* that it works and is real. They know.

XVI

WHEN HYPOCRISY BEGUILES

EVERY decent man and woman detests a hypocrite. Evil is a nasty and nauseous thing at any time, but when it puts on the cloak of piety and uses the language of religion, it is as poisonous a perversion as we are likely to meet a whole long life through. Hypocrisy doubles all the crimes it covers. To lie, to steal, to seduce, to oppress —all these are hateful things, but to engineer them behind a screen of religion is to get the sweetest thing in the universe a bad name. That is why the Church so dreads the hypocrite: he sets her in a false light; he confuses light and darkness in the minds of men outside.

Fécamp Abbey is one of the most interesting ecclesiastical buildings in France. It was built in the twelfth century and has a spacious and noble interior. Its magnificent memorials and tombs entice visitors from all parts of Europe.

The chief charm of the Abbey, however, is its glorious stained-glass windows. If they do not rival the windows at Chartres, they are nevertheless among the most beautiful examples of the stainer's art, and in 1928 the custodians of this old building gave instructions for their precious glass to be removed, restored, and cleaned. But a terrible deception was worked upon them by the expert who undertook the work. She completed the task, but, just before the time came for putting the glass back, was tempted with the sum of Fr. 58,000, to substitute an imitation and sell the Abbey glass to America. She fell. The true glass crossed the Atlantic; a counterfeit was put up in its place; for six years the church was seen in a false light; mysteriously the old glory departed, and no one seemed to know why.

Hypocrites are like that. They set the Church in a false light. The glory of God is best seen on this earth when it streams through a sincere and lovely character, but when it lights on a humbug, it is a strangely distorted beam which gets through. None can deny that hypocrisy partly explains the terrible paralysis which has fallen upon the Church in her prosperous ages. If Christians had been utterly sincere and single-minded it cannot be doubted that the kingdoms of this world would long since have become the kingdom of our God and of his Christ.

Nevertheless, it is important in dealing with this subject to make a few distinctions. The word "hypocrisy" is used very loosely. People fling it about as a term of general contempt without any appreciation of its real meaning. Indeed, there are some peculiarly unpleasant people who call anybody who is striving to live the white life "a hypocrite." It is what the psychologist would call "a defense mechanism." Their own lives are challenged and rebuked by the better life of someone else, and they thrust the challenge aside by saying "hypocrite." They judge themselves. The measure they have meted shall be measured to them again.

Some people have been called "hypocrites" with a show of justification who never deserved the term at all. In a world where thought develops and truth dawns slowly, many men have sincerely held false ideas without clearly seeing that they were false. For instance, in the great battle for the freeing of the slaves many good men candidly believed that slavery was right. They read in their Bibles that Abraham, Isaac, and Jacob kept slaves, and that Paul sent a runaway slave back to his master. Having had some contact with Negroes themselves, they sincerely considered them vastly inferior to white men, and concluded honestly and earnestly that slavery was within the will of God.

Some of the people who were working for the emancipation of the slaves called their opponents "utter hypocrites." Their citation of the Bible was offered as an illustration of Shakespeare's dictum that the Devil can quote scripture when it suits him, and they implied that the defenders of slavery knew the truth and deliberately denied it. In many instances the imputation was unfair. Unmistakably wrong as these men were, they were not conscious hypocrites. Early training and limited thinking trapped them into error, but the best of them were honestly mistaken and the men who called them "hypocrites" were guilty of the sin of slander.

It is probable that the time will come when the Christian conscience will condemn all killing as plain murder —even killing in war. Within a measurable distance of time, the counsel of Christ to love your enemies and do good to them that hate you will be taken seriously, and any man who takes a rifle and fixed bayonet and goes out to disembowel another will be regarded, not as a hero, but as a hired assassin. But that time is not yet. Some of the keenest thinkers in the Church, and some with the tenderest consciences too, are so troubled about aggression and concerned with security that they cannot believe as yet that all war is wrong, and the men who call them "hypocrites" are guilty of the sin of slander.

Nor is it less true in matters of economics. A system which exalts profits above personality is evil and stands condemned, but it is not easy quickly to convert a system which has become the framework of the business world and substitute another. Nor is it just to accuse a man who honestly succeeds under the old system of being a hypocrite. Sir William Hartley, the jam manufacturer, amassed an immense fortune, much of which he gave away with great liberality. He built almshouses and orphanages, a college and a hospital. He gave just, and sometimes generous wages, and was a pioneer of profit sharing. Nevertheless, he was once accused of paying such poor wages to his women employees that he forced them to a life of immorality, a statement born in jealousy and spite, and having no basis in fact. Inquiry has proved that he paid twenty to forty per cent more for female labor than his competitors, and had voluntarily distributed at the time of his death £145,000 in profit sharing to his employees.[1] His accusers said that he was a hypocrite, but the world rightly judged that his accusers were liars. The very foulness of hypocrisy should make responsible men hesitant to use the term freely. If it is indeed a deadly leprosy of the soul, we must be certain that our diagnosis is accurate before we put the label on.

We come closer to the problem when we seek to

---

[1] *Sir William Hartley*, Peake, p. 74.

analyze real hypocrisy in the mind of the hypocrite himself. Hypocrisy is seldom fully conscious. There have been, and doubtless there still are, scheming scoundrels who, without any interest in spirituality at all, learn its language in order to cloak their rascality from honest men; who, like the kite, soar into the blue of heaven, but whose only interest is in some piece of offal on the earth, and who know all the time why they are doing it, and offer no excuses even to themselves. But such instances are very rare. Usually, the hypocrite has a bit of real religion in him but he will not allow it to rule his life. Like the sanctimonious pawnbroker for whom William Booth worked in his early days, he believes "in the Divinity of Jesus Christ and in the Church of which he is a member, but seems to be utterly ignorant of either the theory or practice of experimental godliness." [2]

Quite often, the hypocrite has a profound regard for piety and knows he owes obeisance to it. That was what led La Rochefoucauld to define hypocrisy as "the homage which vice pays to virtue" and almost moves us to a fleeting sympathy with this tormented man. If religion had no grip on him at all, he could end pretense and be a cheerful devil. If Christ possessed his heart entirely, he would know the peace that passes all understanding. As it is, he oscillates between appearance and reality, and finally resolves the interior conflict by self-deception. He becomes in fact an actor. That was the original meaning of the word "hypocrite"—but he lives the part. He does not deny principles, but he admits

[2] *William Booth*, Begbie, Vol. I, p. 81.

exceptions. He firmly holds that immorality is wrong, but, seeing that conditions are not favorable to his marriage . . . or having regard to the sickness, or absence, or temperamental peculiarity of his wife. . . . He freely admits that the money he took was not his own, but, seeing that circumstances alter cases, and that he meant to put it back when he could. . . . He does not deny that the puritan mind might describe that bit of business procedure as a mass of deceit and lies, but, having regard to the stress of business today, and his responsibilities toward his wife and children. . . . So his fatal sophistry goes on, never contradicting the principle but freely excusing himself until, by constant repetition, he comes to believe his own lie, and gets a spurious release from the restlessness of a divided heart.

And if any man of blunt honesty is disposed to brush these mental processes aside and insist that all hypocrisy is a conscious sin, he will merely display his ignorance of psychology. Only as we are willing to follow the tortuous windings of the hypocrite's mind can we understand how he reached this perilous place and how he can heatedly defend himself in the most heinous sins.

Edmund Gosse gives a pitiful instance in *Father and Son*. He tells of a man associated with the religious society to which his father belonged who had "a welcoming wheedling manner and was extremely fluent and zealous in using the pious phraseology of the sect." Edmund Gosse calls him Mr. Dormant. This man received into his home as a paying guest an aged gentleman of much wealth, who died soon after, leaving almost his entire fortune to Mr. Dormant although he had a son, to whom he was much attached, living abroad. But in the passing of time this son returned home, made a few inquiries, and took such steps as lodged Mr. Dormant in prison, and when the trial was heard it came out in evidence "that Dormant had traced the signature to the will by drawing the finger of the testator over the document when he was already and finally coma-tose." Even in court he maintained, to the obvious anger of the judge, that he had only done his duty in trying to divert so much money from being spent in the evil pleasures of the world, and his final statement from the dock declared that he was conscious of his Lord's presence whispering, "Well done, thou good and faith-ful servant."

But, even after all that, Edmund Gosse could not believe that the man was a deliberate and fully conscious hypocrite. With no disposition to defend the religious ideas of the people among whom he had spent his youth, he could, nevertheless, enter into the contortions and rationalizations of this kind of mind, and he knew how they could so palter with moral distinctions that, in the end, the conscience was drugged and they believed a lie.

But to what does all this vacillation lead? It leads, at the last, to the worst state of man. The heart of the hypocrite's sin is here, that he blurs for himself and other people the sharp distinction between right and wrong. He juggles with principles and exceptions until his conscience will not act, even in plain instances, with speed and precision. He calls white black, and black white, and comes to believe it himself. Ultimately, it is the unpardonable sin, and drew forth the most terrible invective that ever fell from the lips of Jesus. We never see the blazing "anger of the lamb" more hot than when we see it dealing with hypocrisy. Not that it is the sin itself which is so deadly, but its insulation from correction. You cannot *shame* it: that is its foul uniqueness. Shame, as the Stoics knew so well, is the basis of all morality. When Jesus appeared to deal so calmly with the sins of impulse and passion and so heatedly with the sin of hypocrisy, it was not that he weighed one sin against the other and found it less evil, but a normal sinner can be shamed, and a hypocrite cannot. He has tampered with the compass of the moral life. If he persists in his evil course, he cannot be saved. He has induced a state of moral myopia which affects his vision even when he looks at Calvary.

Is the position, then, of the hypocrite hopeless? By no means. Grave as it is, it is not beyond the power of Jesus. In the days of his flesh, he seems to have dealt with hypocrisy in two ways: sometimes by fierce denunciation, cutting his way to the conscience by barbed words which were meant to bite through all pretense and bring the hypocrite into the world of honest moral judgment again, and sometimes by the strategy of parables.

There are, of course, the very strictest limits to the use of denunciation, especially in dealing with hypocrisy. It soon palls. Minds are barricaded against it. Nothing so swiftly puts one on the defensive. A touch of overstatement, and the heat of its delivery, often gives the hypocrite all the excuse he wants for putting it aside as a vast exaggeration. Too often it never gets beyond

those areas of his mind where right and wrong are perilously blurred.

But no one ever guarded himself against a simple
story. Consequently, the hypocritical reasonings of a
man's mind can sometimes be circumvented by a naïve
parable, and his drugged conscience revitalized by a
homely narrative, the meaning of which he does not
suspect until it is in possession of his heart. That was
how God saved David when hypocrisy beguiled him.
Nathan came and talked about a man whose little ewe
lamb had been stolen, and the prophet's holy guile outwitted the devil in the heart of David. That was how
Jesus began to deal with his hearers after he had been
accused of being an agent of Beelzebub, and he saw to
what awful lengths their hypocrisy might go. It would
not only pervert: it would persecute. And so by terrible denunciation and warning, and by the use of parables, he sought to save men from the hypocrite's hell.

How does he seek now to save these self-deluded men
and women? Sometimes he is able to draw them into a
Christian fellowship of the very highest quality, an
atmosphere of gracing and uncompromising virtue. In
contact with disciples so simple and sincere, the hypocrite may be arrested in his casuistical course and his conscience orientated afresh. It is no slight achievement
to learn how to be strict in the use of words. The first
steps toward hypocrisy are taken when we ferret about
for a soft word to name an evil thing. Even in childhood we excuse our own lies by calling them "fibs," and
if this process goes on unchecked it blunts the moral
sense. A man is wisely counseled never to call adultery

"love"; call it "adultery": never to call stealing "borrowing," "scrounging," "boning," or any other of those absurd terms which masquerade as synonyms; call it "stealing": never to call deceit and lies "good business"; call it "deceit and lies." A careful use of words in our conversations with ourselves would be a buttress to sincerity.

Sometimes the hypocrites are saved by public exposure. Bitter as the experience is for the hypocrite and damaging to the Church, it may yet issue in the salvation of his soul, against which the contempt of society is a trifle to mention. It depends how far the disease has gone. In a chronic case a man will still defend his dissemblings against the whole world, but it sometimes happens that the weight, and scorn, and unanimity of public opinion, carries conviction to his heart and he comes, by way of shame and penitence, to forgiveness. I remember one such instance myself. After the awful exposure and the deep penitence it engendered, the man continued to live in the same small country town where everyone knew his story but came again to a sincere respect for him. He was a devout disciple when he died, and his end was peace.

A sudden view of the Cross has startled some hypocrites back to sincerity. The five bleeding wounds are so *real*. The naked body sagging on the pierced hands shatters pretense. Holding up the Cross, a preacher may still prove Christ's power to draw men unto him, the hypocrite with the rest.

Finally, it may be said quite simply that in some mysterious way, and by some mystic experience, Christ sometimes arrests the hypocrite in a manner for which no ordinary explanation can be given. Such an instance is in my mind as I write. The subject of the experience has told me the vivid story many times: a vision of Jesus which barred his path and a glance of those searching majestic eyes that seemed to rip all the guilty secrets from his bosom. Then a tense word which conveyed to his mind that Jesus was offering him one more chance, and scalding tears started from his eyes. So he found his way back to sincerity. Repentance, confession, restitution, and much prayer were the steps by which he picked his path to peace. He always speaks of himself as a man who has been to the very brink of Hell. He has. Hypocrisy shares with pride the unpleasant distinction of being a very direct road to perdition.

XVII

WHEN BIGOTRY BANISHES LOVE

DESPITE certain sayings in the New Testament which might be quoted against the view, it cannot be seriously doubted that bigotry was abhorrent to Jesus Christ. On one occasion he made his will on the subject unforgettably clear. The Apostle John burst in on him and said: "Master, we saw one casting out devils in thy name, and we forbade him because he followeth not with us," and Jesus rebuked the Son of Thunder in no uncertain way.

One wonders what John expected that Jesus would say. He made the announcement in the manner of a man rather pleased with his promptitude. He told the story as though he anticipated some praise for his zeal. *Casting out devils?* But, surely, that was a good thing to do: banishing demons, and bringing demented men and women back to their normal minds. It was a mission of mercy, to be encouraged at all costs. *In thy name.* Better still! He commanded the demons in the authoritative name of Jesus and he made no secret as to where his authority lay. *And we forbade him . . . because he followed not with us.* The pity of it. The narrowness and bigotry, and intolerance of it. Jesus said: "Forbid him not; for he that is not against us is for us."

The spirit of bigotry did not die with Apostolic times. It is not dead yet. Few words in the New Testament have been more neglected than our Lord's rebuke of bigotry. All through the ages one group of disciples has been forbidding others on no more serious ground than that "he followeth not with us." No one familiar with history and jealous for the honor of the Christian religion, can help feeling unutterably sad when they read the story of religious persecution. The burning and torturing of Protestants in one reign, and the torturing and burning of Roman Catholics in another, and all undertaken in the name of Christ who said, "Love thy neighbor as thyself."

Nor is it all *ancient* history. Though persecutions are less common than once they were, the poisoned word is still flung about, and men wound one another in the tenderest part of their soul, and think that they do God service in so doing. Expressions of blind and bitter bigotry are not unknown even today.

Sir Arthur Conan Doyle was born a Roman Catholic and was educated by the Jesuits. He says:

"I have a kindly feeling toward all Jesuits. I see now both their limitations and their virtues. They have been slandered in some things, for during eight years of constant contact I cannot remember that they were less truthful than their fellows, or more casuistical than their neighbors."

But he also says:

"Nothing can exceed the uncompromising bigotry of the Jesuit theology, or their apparent ignorance of how it shocks the modern conscience. I remember that when, as a grown lad, I heard Father Murphy, a great fierce Irish priest, declare that there was sure damnation for everyone outside the Church, I looked upon him with horror, and to that moment

I trace the first rift which has grown into such a chasm between me and those who were my guides."[1]

"Sure damnation for everyone outside the Roman Church"? Did Father Murphy know nothing of the saints of other communions? Had he never heard of Richard Baxter and George Herbert; of Josephine Butler and Catherine Booth; of John Keble and Frank Crossley; of Charles Haddon Spurgeon and C. T. Studd; of George Müller and Alexander Whyte—these and a thousand others like them, all outside the Roman Church, but who cast out the devils of sin, and lived lives that were lovely, and did it all in the name of Christ? Sure damnation? Why? Is it simply because "they follow not with us"?

But the Roman Church has no monopoly of bigotry. Protestantism knows how to be bitter in opposition. No one will doubt it who has heard the heartiness with which an Orangeman says, "To hell with the Pope," or seen anything of the riots which sometimes mark the celebration of the Battle of the Boyne in Liverpool. One wonders if these hot zealots know anything of the saints of Rome; not merely those officially recognized as saints but others also, whose lives were winsome in holiness, or who, like their Lord, went about doing good; St. Francis of Assisi, and Brother Lawrence; Jean-Marie Vianney, and Father Damien; Charles de Foucauld, and Baron von Hugel, and many, many more on whom God set the seal of his approval, and who walked with him in white. How can one speak other than gratefully and reverently

[1] *Memoirs and Adventures*, Conan Doyle, pp. 26 f.

of such rare and humbling souls, even though it be true that they "follow not with us"?

Not, of course, that any vast question of truth can be proved by character. While it is true, in a broad sense, that "by their fruits ye shall know them," one may not justly reason from the holiness of a man's life to the truth of all his ideas. Many a false belief has been propagated by a good man, and his goodness made the falsity of his ideas the more dangerous, because the ideas received a currency which would have been denied to the creed of a baser man. A communion may produce saints and yet be in error in its teaching. Buddhism has had its saints, and claims the honorable distinction of being the only great religion which has not sought to spread itself by murder, but that does not prove the truth of Buddhism, or the superiority and completeness of its creed. Not all the saints in the Roman Calendar would convince an ardent Protestant of the doctrine of papal infallibility, nor all the saints of Protestantism convince a Roman Catholic of the right of private judgment. Goodness is not logic, nor piety proof, nor sanctity reason. Beyond and above all the fine fruits of holiness in consecrated human lives, and which appear in such compelling loveliness in so many communions, the questions of ultimate truth still invite solution. No creed can be wholly wrong which produces saints, but neither need it be completely true on that ground alone. The citation of saints cannot finally settle questions of truth. That must freely be conceded on all sides before we can discover the real core of the bigot's sin.

Bigotry is not to be confused with a firm grasp of

truth, as one has understood it. Such firmness of conviction is expected in all men of mature mind. People of elastic principles and nebulous beliefs neither deserve, nor receive, the respect of normal men. It is surely to be expected that when one has come to faith through much mental stress, and one's faith has proved itself a mainstay through all the chances and changes of this mortal life, that one should hold to it firmly, tenaciously even. Real religion needs more than a clot of vague sentiment at its core: it requires a body of definite belief which one is ready to guard with one's life.

Bigotry intrudes when, not content with guarding one's own faith with one's life, men will rob another man of his life because his faith is not the same. The disposition to persecute is nearly always attached to bigotry. Circumstances may prevent it finding any fiercer expression than a barbed tongue can command, but intolerance is there and, quite often, the will to wound.

Moreover, bigotry neglects the fact that truth has many facets, and can be seen in different lights. If a man said that a robot has a red light, he would be stating the simple truth, but so would a man who said that it had a green light, and so would a man who said that it was sometimes yellow. The bigot ignores this truth. He sees one light and denies the presence of the others. He cannot, or will not, believe that other men are as sincere in their affirmations as he is sincere himself.

Furthermore, he does not realize that so unreasoning a thing as temperament plays a not unimportant part in religious differences. Edward Byles Cowell used to stress this point in his efforts to explain to Hindus the difference between the Church of England and "Dissenters." He said that the distinction belonged to the realm of *feeling* rather than *conscience,* the lovers of institutionalism and antiquity preferring the former, and the lovers of reform the latter. We need not concede that this is a full statement of the differences, nor yet an accurate one of the points which it stresses, to admit that temperament, as well as the accident of birth, does play a part in the problem which bigotry thrusts upon us all.

But this, of course, cannot clear up the differences. When every allowance has been made for the various angles of vision, and the changing light in which truth may be seen, and the differences of temperament, there still remain some divergences of belief which cannot be dissipated in this way. It seems certain that if one communion is right on some points, the others are wrong. Willingness to concede that *possibility* ought to be in the mind of every sincere seeker of truth. It is astonishing how much more reasonable the view of an opponent appears if one really listens patiently to its careful statement and tries to enter into it in his way. But when one's fellowship is limited to people of the same view, and such occasional discussions as are possible with members of another communion are lost in foolish efforts to make debating points, the day of understanding is indefinitely postponed.

And that brings us to the hateful heart of the bigot's sin, namely, that he fails in love. It is not wrong, but a plain duty, to reason with those who have not seen the truth as we have seen it. Being willing to listen to their view, we must be ready also to state our own, and persuasively and convincingly set out the truth we have received and on which our hope rests.

But if we disagree, Christ is able to help us disagree without being disagreeable. If we still differ, he can aid us that we do not lapse from affection. It cannot surprise him that earnest and honest men differ in their explanations of the holy mysteries of the faith, but it must pain him when those who call themselves by his name clearly fail in love.

"But what are we to do," people ask, "when others fail in love toward us; when they speak contemptuously of beliefs so dear that we would die for them; when they deride our doctrines, and pour scorn on our sanctities; when they say that we are not in the old Church, or the real Church, or the true Church, or even in the Church at all?"

The answer is not hard, though the practice often is. One must go on loving. One must meet slander with affection, scorn with service, pride with humility, and excommunication with the right hand of fellowship. We are followers of him who said, "He that is not against us is for us"; who, being reviled, reviled not again; who met all the indignities of persecuting bigots with meekness, and died praying for their pardon. Love is the only permissible answer. It cannot solve questions of truth, but it can create the atmosphere in which alone truth can be seen. No ecclesiastical writ can really unchurch a devout believer who can love in the spirit of Jesus, for those who love most are nearest God, for God is love.

Nor is there any lack of encouragement for those who long for closer communion with all who love our Lord. The nearer we come to the Cross, the nearer we come to one another. Explanations divide us, but our religious experience constantly draws us together. The language of devotion respects no barriers. Prayers and hymns which have been born in one branch of the Holy Catholic Church are often used, without any sense of incongruity, in other branches of the Church also.

Moreover, it cannot be denied that the indebtedness extends still further, and includes the spiritual preparation of some who have become leaders in other communions than the one into which they were born. It has been customary in time past to speak or think with pain of the "apostasy" of those distinguished men who have left the Church of their fathers to become pillars in some other temple, but surely there is ground for gratitude that God was able to use them so well. No religious leader can entirely divorce himself from his early spiritual training. His effectiveness for God runs back in large part to the communion which first nourished him in holy things, and this traffic through the barriers is a witness to an underlying catholicity and the herald of a better day to come.

Cardinals Manning and Newman were both cradled in the Anglican Church. The Anglican Church gave Wesley to the Methodists, and the Methodists partly repaid the debt in the first Bishop of Chelmsford, and the present Bishop of Truro. Both came from Methodist homes. Spurgeon, the mighty Baptist preacher, was converted in a Methodist Chapel, and William Booth, the founder of the Salvation Army, was a Methodist minister. The present Archbishop of Canterbury received his early religious training in the Presbyterian Church. Many more instances of this movement between the denominations could be given, and while it is true that some converts become bitter bigots, it is probable that these exchanges will tend, as time passes, to interpret the mind of one communion to another and hasten the day when, having one Shepherd, we shall be one flock.

Outspoken utterances by responsible leaders foster the thought. Earlier in this chapter we had occasion to quote a bigoted utterance of a Jesuit priest, but it is possible to place beside that a more recent statement from a similar source, and on the same subject. Father Woodlock, the well-known Jesuit from the Farm Street Church in London, expressed horror, in a widely-published interview, that he should be suspected of the view that only Roman Catholics go to heaven. He said:

"I expect to meet Anglicans and Nonconformists, Unitarians and Presbyterians, Arians and Plymouth Brethren, and all those who, through no fault of their own, have never known and never rejected Christ, and have been helped by grace to love God and repent of sin. . . ." [2]

"How could one ever smile again," he continued, "if, in a country like this, I thought God's grace came only to our three million Catholics in a total population of nearly fifty millions?" [3]

[2] *One Thing I Know*, A. J. Russell, p. 335.
[3] *Ibid.*, p. 338.

The spirit of charity which breathes through this confident expectation contrasts sharply with the "sure damnations" of Father Murphy, and proves that Rome's proud claim *semper eadem* is not meant to limit the outpourings of Divine love.

Even in the worst ages of bigotry, there were lovely deeds of magnanimous affection which shine like jewels in the dark story of the past. When Richard Baxter, the Puritan divine, was condemned at the age of seventy by the notorious Judge Jeffreys, after a most unjust trial, he was befriended by a Roman Catholic peer. Flung into prison until he could pay the impossible fine of five hundred marks, he might have languished there till he died but for the unwearying exertions of Lord Powis, by which he was at last set at liberty. Baxter was a great lover of tolerance himself. It is sweet to think that he tasted something of its fruits before he died.

Such kindliness multiplies as the years go by. Despite the forces which oppose it, the spirit of Jesus wins its widening way and, in new circumstances, new expressions are found.

In September, 1917, Albert Schweitzer was snatched away from his noble medical work in West Africa, to be interned as a German subject, by the French. It was one of the minor senseless tragedies of the war. Just as they were hurrying him on to the river boat to take him to the coast, the Father Superior of the Catholic Mission appeared. Waving aside with an authoritative gesture all the native soldiers who tried to prevent him boarding the boat, he took Schweitzer and his wife by the hand

and said: "You shall not leave this country without my thanking you both for all the good that you have done it." [4] It was a simple courtesy, but those Protestant prisoners felt it like a healing balm.

Dr. Orchard has publicly stated that nothing comforted him so much in the anxious weeks which preceded his crossing to Rome than the letters from his Nonconformist friends, which were so full of trust and confidence, and the promise of perpetual friendship and unchanging affection even in an impending decision which ran directly counter to their own strongly-held convictions. [5]

The final banishment of bigotry may still be far away, but we welcome the signs of its passing, and insist that it is upon these things that the stress should fall rather than on the evidence of its survival. Faith in the triumph of love, and a readiness to tell of conquests already won, will extend its sway still more, and hasten the time for which the devout work and pray, when his dismembered Body shall be whole again.

Let us conclude with a picture of two Churches. In the town of Glarus in Switzerland, the population is both Protestant and Roman Catholic. They use the same church. A curtain is drawn across the Roman Catholic altar at the conclusion of Mass and, as the worshipers leave, they say "Good morning" to their Protestant neighbors who are coming in. It does not seem strange to the people. The custom of other Cantons

---

[4] *Out of My Life and Thought*, Albert Schweitzer, p. 194. Henry Holt and Company, publishers.

[5] *From Faith to Faith*, Orchard, p. 171.

seems strange to them. Perhaps it seems strange to God also.

In the town of Arundel in Sussex, the parish church is bricked up at the chancel arch. The nave is Anglican, the chancel is Roman Catholic: One church with a dividing wall. How odd it seems! It happened like this. When the rift with Rome came in England, the Duke of Norfolk, whose seat is near by, remained loyal to the older communion and claimed the chancel of the parish church, in which his ancestors were buried, as his private property. His claim was honored, and the chancel arch was bricked up. But that was many years ago. The wall is old, and looks its age. One has gazed upon it many times and thought of its parabolic significance. The wall between! But some day it will fall. Did not Jesus pray that all those which believe on him may be one? And can Jesus pray in vain? And is he not able to hasten that day, with every new heart which is really given to him, until, at last, all sing with Charles Wesley:

> "Love, like death, hath all destroyed,
> Rendered all distinctions void;
> Names, and sects, and parties fall:
> Thou, O Christ, art all in all."